THE BLOOD

THE BLOOD

Paul Fenwick

First published in 2021

ISBN: 978-1-9997038-3-7

DEDICATION

I dedicate this book to my wife Linda (thirty-nine years married at the time of writing). Your love, patience and wisdom still continue to amaze me! As my wife and my best friend, let our journey together continue onward and upward!

Contents

ACKNOWLEDGEMENTS

Firstly I would like to say a big "thank you" to Linda (my wife of forty years) for taking my scribbling and translating them into readable English (you are amazing)!

Also, I would like to thank Nicola who took the notes every week and faithfully printed them out, and finally "thank you" to everyone at BCFI who have encouraged me throughout the time it has taken me to write this book!

You are all amazing!

INTRODUCTION

This book (THE BLOOD) has been forming in the womb of my spirit for thirty-five years (August 1985 – October 2020), a very long pregnancy!

After writing the booklet "Developing the Royal Gift of Tongues", it was suggested to me (on a number of occasions) that I should write a book. As I look back, all these suggestions were really the HOLY SPIRIT nudging me in a certain direction.

If I was asked to describe this book, my reply would be, "This book is a container full of seeds. We all know that a seed looks nothing like the end product, but without the seed there won't be an end product!"

So, with total reliance on the Holy Spirit, I pray that this book, "THE BLOOD", will make you more and more hungry for greater and deeper revelation and experiences that are in "THE BLOOD", and that come through the Blood, and the sower (HOLY SPIRIT) will sow multitudes of BLOOD SEED into the good ground of your heart, so that in your life you will encounter continual, experiential revelation about

"THE BLOOD!"

"The Life is in the Blood!"

"The Keys are in the Blood!"

"Study the Blood!"

1

In the Beginning

My first beginning started (according to my birth certificate) on the 22nd May 1955 in a Maternity Hospital in the east end of my City.

My second beginning happened on the 10th August 1985 (thirty years later in the house of a well respected man of God (Robert Ward), who was an Apostle with a powerful preaching, teaching and deliverance ministry). That was the day I was born of the Spirit and washed in the Blood of the Lamb!
From death into life! From darkness into light!
From sickness into health! From the curse into the blessing! From poverty into prosperity! All because of the Blood of Jesus!

"The Life is in the Blood!"

At the time of my conversion (new birth), I had no knowledge, understanding or conscious awareness of "The Blood of the Son of Man" (John 6:53), "The Blood of the New Covenant" (Matthew 26:28), "The Blood of the Cross" (Colossians 1:20), "The Blood of Jesus" (Hebrews 10:19), or "The Blood of the Lamb" (Revelation 7:14; 12:11).

The next night (11th August 1985) I was baptised in the Holy Spirit and fire and spoke in Tongues.

"The Life is in the Blood!"

The first spiritual contraction connected to the birthing of this book, "The Blood", happened (as far as I can remember) in 1987 when I was given access to a video called "A Blood Washed Africa" featuring an Evangelist (who I had never heard of) called Reinhard Bonnke. So I turned the video player on and sat down to watch "A Blood Washed Africa". What I saw and heard in that short thirty minute video cut me to the heart. The tears ran down my face as I saw the Holy Spirit move in amazing power and demonstration, but what reached into my heart and hooked me, spirit, soul and body, was Reinhard Bonnke preaching and talking about "The Blood of Jesus" and "A Blood Washed Africa". A whole continent washed in the "Blood of Jesus"! I didn't hear any call to Africa, but I was gripped and consumed by the anointed message on "The Blood". The seed had been planted!

"The Life is in the Blood!"

Contraction number two came in 1995 when the Holy Spirit directed me to record on a forty-five minute cassette tape as many of the Promises that are in the Word of God that concern the righteous and righteousness, and to reproduce them and to give them out to as many as would receive them (it was quite a task). I believed to start with Psalm 1:6, "The Lord knows the way of the righteous", and finish with Revelation 19:9, "Blessed are those called to the Marriage Supper of the Lamb"!

"The Life is in the Blood!"

In the year 2000, at the end of one of our meetings, I was approached by someone who told me that she had a vision of my rib cage and vertebrae, which had been replaced with books of all different sizes and types. Some were hardback, some were paperbacks, plus there were booklets and pamphlets. At that time, writing books, booklets and pamphlets had never entered my mind, so I responded the same way as Sarah did when she was told she was going to have a son, "I laughed!" So here I am, after writing the booklet "Developing the Royal Gift of Tongues", writing a book on "The Blood"!

Contraction number three came in September 2005. A very good friend of mine, Tom Leighton, gave me a book to read called "The Blood of the Cross" by Andrew Murray (1828-1917). In my own natural understanding I found this book hard to grasp, but to my spirit it was like fresh rain in the desert.

"The Life is in the Blood!"

Contraction number four came in November 2005. I heard very clearly in my spirit from the Holy Spirit, "The Keys are in the Blood!"

This speaks to me of keys of revelation, keys of victory, health, prosperity, favour and many, many more, but the statement, "The Keys are in the Blood" tells me exactly what I must focus on, "The Blood!" In Joshua 1:8 (this is one of my life scriptures) it basically says:

1. Do not let God's Word depart from your mouth!
2. Meditate on it day and night!
3. Do what it says!
4. You will prosper and have good success!

So, statement number one is to "speak out by faith what the Word says and what you believe in your heart about "The Blood"!"

Statement number two is "keep your mind, will and emotions continually fixed and focussed on what "The Blood" has done, is doing and will eternally do for you, day and night!"

Statement number three, "Do what it says" (Isaiah 1:19), because faith without corresponding works (actions, lifestyle) is dead! So the outcome of focussing on "The Blood", applying "The Keys that are in the Blood" is statement number four, "prosperity and good success!"

If you are one of these strange Christians who doesn't want to prosper and be successful, then I suggest you stop reading this book, stay away from the Word of God and do not go near the Blood of Jesus, but if you want to prosper in all things, be in excellent health and have a restored soul (3 John 1:2), then plunge your mind, by faith, into "The Blood of Jesus" and stay submerged until you come out with some keys!

Contraction number five happened on the 1st November 2014. The Holy Spirit said very clearly, "The Father does not want the Blood of His Son hidden or concealed, He wants it revealed and released!"

These types of encounters in my experience are always accompanied by "The Spirit of the Fear of the Lord" (Isaiah 11:2; 3a, Revelation 1:4; 4:5; 5:6) and, although I didn't understand how to do this or walk it out on a daily basis, my answer was, "Yes, here I am, send me!"

Contraction number six happened on the 5th June 2015 (in the room I'm sitting in now writing this book). On that day I was praying in Tongues when a "voice" (Acts 10:13a) spoke to me very loudly, clearly, authoritatively, and the voice said,

"Study the Blood!"

(The devil will never tell you to do that!) Although that was quite an experience in itself, I did not hear the audible "voice" in my ears, I heard "Study the Blood" in my eyes, very clearly. To try to explain this encounter in English is impossible, but it is my testimony and it was a real time event!

So now we can put these three statements together:

"The Life is in the Blood!"

"The Keys are in the Blood!"
"Study the Blood!"

Contraction number seven came a month later at 10.30am on the 7th July 2015, I heard very early (in my mind):

"GET THE BLOOD TO THE BODY!"

A body that is not getting enough blood is termed anaemic. Some of the symptoms of anaemia are fatigue, physical weakness, shortness of breath and dizziness.

As I sit writing this book on "The Blood", and I look back at the condition of the Body of Christ in my City, Region and Nation at that time (2015), all the signs of anaemia were there, but because there was no negative pressure being put on the Body, it was not obvious, but now (October 2020), the anaemic state and the symptoms of anaemia in the Body of Christ here in my City, Region and Nation are extremely obvious (Isaiah 13:6; 42:22, Hosea 7:9, Amos 3:11).

"We must get the Blood to the Body!"

The Holy Spirit is calling for volunteers!

"Revelation 12:11"

Contraction number eight came at the latter part of 2017 when someone approached me at the end of a meeting and said, "You should write a book on The Blood!" Once again I heard the Holy Spirit speaking!

Contraction number nine happened on the 26th February 2019. Once again I heard the Holy Spirit say, "Walk through the Realms of My Blood!" I did not know it then but I do now, that the statement, "Walk through the Realms of My Blood" was and is multidimensional!

(At this point I would like to point out that, although Satan is very experienced in misinformation and misdirection and his kingdom is a counterfeit kingdom, he cannot counterfeit "The Blood".)

"The Life is in the Blood!"
"The Keys are in the Blood!"
"Study the Blood!"
"Walk through the Realms of the Blood!"

Contraction number ten happened in September 2020. I was sitting relaxing, praying in Tongues (one of the ways the Holy Spirit works in my life is to put me in two or more realities at the same time). So, as I'm praying in Tongues in a room in my house, I am also in another reality at the same time (bi-location) (both realities are equally as real). In this other reality, I am standing looking at a very large golden bowl which is brim full of bright red blood, and as I am looking at this golden bowl full of blood, a voice said, "The Keys are in the Blood" (so this is the second time I've been told this, the first time was in November 2005). As I'm looking at the golden bowl full of blood, I think, "How do I get the keys out?" Immediately the answer came (twice), "You've got to reach in. You've got to reach in." (Two is the number of agreement.) So, in this other reality (remember I'm also sitting at home praying in Tongues), I reach into the blood filled bowl, and as my hand and arm go into the blood, I felt a key placed in the palm of my hand, and as I started to pull my arm out of the blood, I was back in my physical three-dimensional reality!

Contraction number eleven happened on the 23rd September 2020. Someone asked me over the internet, "Would I do a teaching, via the internet, on the Armour of God?" This seemed like a reasonable request at the time, but the reply I received from the Holy Spirit was, "The Keys to understanding the Armour of God will come through revelation of The Blood!"

Contraction number twelve happened on the 5th October 2020. I was asked if I would take the Vlog teachings I have been doing on "The Blood" and turn them into a book. So here we are, on the 17th October 2020, at the end of Chapter One on "The Blood".

The Blood of Jesus is not a historical subject to be intellectually studied, but The Blood of Jesus is a living realm and reality to be experienced now!

"The Life is in the Blood!"
"The Keys are in the Blood!"
"Study the Blood!"
"Get the Blood to the Body!"
"Walk through the Realms of My Blood!"

POEM

OH THE BLOOD OF JESUS

(VERSE ONE)

OH THE BLOOD OF JESUS
SPEAKS TO ME TODAY

YES, THE BLOOD OF JESUS
GUIDES ME THROUGH THE DAY

OH THE PRECIOUS BLOOD
HAS CLEANSED ME FROM WITHIN

HALLELUJAH!
THE BLOOD OF JESUS
HAS SET ME FREE FROM THE POWER OF SIN

2

The Life is in the Blood

God (Elohim) activated His Eternal Plan for the redemption and reconciliation of mankind before the conception and foundation of the World (Kosmos). He did this by "slaying a lamb" (Revelation 13:8b), because without Blood, there can be no Redemption or Reconciliation! Therefore, before He created the Heavens, before He created the Archangels, the Cherubim and Seraphim, the Living Creatures, the Angels, the heavenly City of Jerusalem, the plan for mankind's redemption and reconciliation had already been completed in Him!

"Study the Blood!"
"The Keys are in the Blood!"

The blood that continually runs through our veins is an amazing substance. The nature of blood is to return to its original source, its point of origin. So, if you cut yourself with a sharp knife, your blood would drip onto the ground and the ground would soak it up or receive it back! Human blood comes out of the earth. Human blood has a beginning and an end. Human blood is made up of fallen DNA and is subject to the "Law of sin and death" until you get "Born Again", then everything about your life here on earth can change, because "the Law of the Spirit of Life (the Life is in the Blood) in Christ Jesus sets us free from the Law of Sin (fallen DNA, sickness, poverty, fear) and death". Human blood with its fallen DNA ceases to be a problem when we put our Faith in the "Blood of Jesus"!

The Blood of Jesus is the antidote for the venom of the snake and the sting of the scorpion!

"Study the Blood!"
"The Keys are in the Blood!"

The Blood of Jesus was and is eternally different to fallen human blood. The Blood of Jesus did not originate on planet Earth or from anywhere else in our ever expanding universe. The Blood of Jesus came out of Heaven, originated in the Father (who has no beginning or end). So from the garden to the cross, his Blood could not be absorbed by the earth.

"Study the Blood!"

So when Jesus said in John 14:30, that the ruler (ar-khone), prince of this world (Kosmos) (Adam's position before the fall) has nothing in me, He was declaring that His Blood and His body were completely free from fallen DNA. He (Jesus) was the "Perfect, Spotless, Sinless Lamb of God. Jesus did not come out of the earth, He (Jesus) came out of the Father (John 16:28). He was born from above (John 8:23). Satan had no legal right to Him, and because of the "Blood of the Lamb, the Blood of the Cross, and the Blood of the New Covenant", Satan has no legal right to us either. "Hallelujah!"

"Study the Blood!"
"The Keys are in the Blood!"

Everything the Father is, was, or ever will be is incorporated in the Blood of His Son, Jesus, our Redeemer, our Saviour, our King! We are in an eternal Blood Covenant (Hebrews 13:20) with Almighty God, that makes us and our lives here on earth (in the visible and the invisible) His personal responsibility (John 15:16). The Blood Covenant that we have entered into cannot be improved upon or diminished in any way. It is completely complete! So the Blood of Jesus will continually avail for us here on earth!

"The Life is in the Blood!"
"Study the Blood!"
"The Keys are in the Blood!"

The Blood of the Lamb is the Eternal (Revelation 13:8b) foundation of our Redemption (Ephesians 1:7a), our Reconciliation (Colossians 1:20), our Righteousness (Romans 5:9a), our Sanctification (Hebrews 13:12a).

The Blood of the Lamb is the reason we can be legally baptised in the Holy Spirit and fire, and continue to be filled with the Holy Spirit on a daily basis.

The Blood of the Lamb gives us free access to the Father (Hebrews 10:19) and all that He is and has, because through the "Blood of Jesus" we are joint heirs with Christ (Romans 8:17a).

"As He is, so are we in this World!"

"The Blood" is a gift of grace to all humanity (if they choose to appropriate it by faith), and you would think the most important foundational subject in the whole of eternity, past, present and future, "the

Blood", would be the most important subject Apostles and Prophets would be preaching about, teaching about, holding seminars and conferences about, and also writing Apostolic/Prophetic books and Praise songs about, but in my own personal experience over the last thirty-five years here in the United Kingdom, Malaysia, The Philippines, Kenya, Nepal, Germany and Norway (places the Lord has taken me to), the Blood was never mentioned or spoken about in any public or private setting!

The question is, "Why has the Blood disappeared from the Church?"

The answer is very simple! "Satan hates the Blood", (Job 1:5,10) and he has slowly and systematically over the last 100 years misdirected the Church away from "the Blood of the Cross, the Blood of Jesus, the Blood of the Lamb, the Blood of the New Covenant", and redirected them on to a multitude of different subjects that have no eternal relevance at all, either here on Earth or in Heaven!

Question: "Why did Satan and his government (Ephesians 6:12) implement this strategy?"

The answer is that "The Blood of Jesus" is the most terrifying and feared substance Satan has ever encountered. He has no defence and is powerless against it! Also "The Blood" is the most feared substance principalities, powers, evil thrones, demons, unclean and wicked spirits have ever encountered or been exposed to. "The Blood of Jesus" terrifies them, paralyses them, overcomes them and humiliates them!

"We Overcome by The Blood of the Lamb!"

"The Blood is a Heavenly Weapon
Atomic in its Power against
the kingdom of darkness!"

"Have Faith in the Blood!"

The Blood of Jesus is the currency of Heaven and all the Heavenly Realms, and is the unstoppable power of redemption. Satan and his kingdom are totally defenceless and powerless where the Blood is concerned. The soul hunters of Isaiah 49:24, Ezekiel 13:18,20 and Revelation 18:13, have to release their hold on the soul, mind and bodies of their captives when the Ecclesia of the King of kings step into the spirit and apply and release "The Blood of the Cross", in Jesus' Name!

"The captives are set free (Isaiah 49:25-26)"
"The Keys are in the Blood!"

The Hymn writer wrote:

"And can it be that I should gain
An interest in my Saviour's Blood?"

Ask the Holy Spirit to give you an ever increasing hunger for fresh revelation and experience in and about the Blood!

There is nothing that comes out of Heaven or the Kingdom of God (visible or invisible) that's not based on the Blood of the Lamb, the Blood of the Cross, the Blood of Jesus or the Blood of the New Covenant, plus all angelic activity (where man is concerned) has to be legal (Hebrews 1:14) and is based on the Blood of the New Covenant, with Jesus being the guarantee (Hebrews 7:22). Remember, whatever is done through the Blood is legal, and Satan has no defence where the Blood is concerned.

"Study the Blood!"

Through the Blood we have been made kings and priests (Revelation 1:6). The Father paid an unimaginable price (Jesus) to open the way so He could get his ultimate creation (man) back into eternal fellowship. The Blood of the Lamb was and still is the redemptive price for the life of a man or woman. So our King Jesus is not impressed in any way with lukewarm, anaemic, passive Christians (Revelation 3:16). He did not send the Holy Spirit at Pentecost to raise up a lukewarm, anaemic, passive church. If natural healthy blood is essential for life and keeping a person young, vibrant and healthy, how much more important is the Blood of Jesus to his collective body or the individual believer?

The Blood of Jesus to the body of Christ is more important than the air we breathe.

The air we breathe, the food we eat and the water we drink are all temporary, but the Blood of Jesus is eternal!

"His Life is in His Blood!"

In 1 Peter 2:9 it says that we are a "Holy Nation!" I was born in the United Kingdom, I am a citizen of the United Kingdom, and I have a UK passport, but that doesn't make me holy, sanctified or set apart. It's the Blood and only the Blood that redeems us, makes us righteous and sanctifies us. It's the Blood that qualifies us to be part of or member of a "Holy Nation!"

- We are sons/daughters because of the Blood!
- We are kings and royal priests in the order of Melchizedek because of the Blood!

- We are Citizens of a Holy Nation because of the Blood!
- We are Saints because of the Blood!
- We are overcomers because of the Blood!

Revelation by the Holy Spirit about all the many facets of the Blood is of national importance to every heavenly citizen here on earth, so that we can walk out our destiny (Psalm 139:16, Jeremiah 1:5a) in the resurrection life and power that is in the Blood, and see and experience the advancement of God's Kingdom in our own personal world and life!

"The Keys are in the Blood!"

Whatever is built on the basis and foundation of the "Blood of Jesus" is built on the Rock (Matthew 7:24-25). If we build anything that is not based on "the Blood", then we are building on sand (2 Timothy 3:5).

- We were bought with His Blood (Acts 20:28)
- We are righteous through His Blood (Romans 5:9)
- We have been set apart through His Blood (Hebrews 13:12)

- We are cleansed by His Blood (1 John 1:7)
- We are in relationship with the seven spirits by His Blood (Revelation 1:4b)
- We overcome by His Blood (Revelation 12:11)

So, let us plunge fearlessly into the truths that are in the Word of God about the Blood from Revelation to Genesis to Revelation. Let us allow the Holy Spirit to teach us and guide us. Let us daily live, move and have our being in the resurrection life and almighty power that is in the Blood of Jesus.

"The Life is in the Blood!"
"The Keys are in the Blood!"
"Study the Blood!"
"Get the Blood to the Body!"

OH THE BLOOD OF JESUS

(VERSE 2)

OH THE BLOOD OF JESUS
IS A FOUNTAIN DEEP AND WIDE

YES, THE BLOOD OF JESUS
BRINGS THE ANGELS TO MY SIDE

OH THE PRECIOUS BLOOD
PROTECTS ME ALONG THE WAY

HALLELUJAH!
THE BLOOD OF JESUS
AVAILS FOR ME TODAY

3

The Untouchables: (Job 1:1-10)

The first untouchable I want to draw your attention to is Job. (I think I need to repeat at this point in the book that if you are one of those strange Christians who doesn't want to prosper and be successful, (Genesis 1:26-31, Genesis 2:11-12, Joshua 1:8, Psalm 1:2-3, Psalm 23:1-3, 2 Corinthians 8:9) then stop reading this book, close your Bible and stay away from the Blood of the Lamb, the Blood of the New Covenant and the Promises of God, which are all "Yes and Amen!") But, if you want to prosper, be successful, have dominion in your life, in your world (sphere of influence), then read on!

"The Keys are in the Blood!"
"Reach in!"

In Job 1:1 we are given the privilege to read a glowing report about Job:

1. He is blameless!
2. He is upright!
3. He fears God.
4. He shuns evil.

(This is an amazing testimony for someone who wasn't Born Again.)

In Job 1:2 we are told that he has seven sons and three daughters (Job 2:9 tells us also that he has a wife).

In Job 1:3 there is a record of all his livestock and animals:

1. Seven thousand sheep.
2. Three thousand camels.
3. Five hundred yolk of oxen.
4. Five hundred female donkeys.

Plus the land, food and water needed to continually care for them, also:

5. A very large household with servants.

In Job 29:7-23 he gives us his own personal and positional testimony about the divine favour of God upon his life.

The conclusion that we can draw from all this Holy Spirit inspired information is that Job was the greatest, richest, wealthiest, most esteemed and most influential and prosperous man of all the people of the east! (Job 1:3)

"Study the Blood!"

In Job 1:4 we see that Job's seven sons and three daughters had their own houses and they were definitely "party people". They ate, drank and partied for days (without being hindered by a religious guilt complex or religious parents). What a great family to belong to!

"Because of the Blood of the New Covenant,
there is NO condemnation in Christ!"

So the burning question is, "What was the key to Job's amazing prosperity, his excellent physical health, his high Governmental position and his tremendous success?"

The answer is in two realities, the visible and the invisible!

In the visible we see the faith and diligence of Job. In Job 1:5 it says that, "He would rise early in the morning" (after his seven sons and three daughters had finished partying), and, "He would offer burnt (fire) offerings (animal sacrifices) for them all." It also says that, "Job would sanctify them". There is only one acceptable way of sanctification in the eyes of God and that is through and by blood. Hebrews 13:12 says that, "He (Jesus) might sanctify the people with His Blood."

Sanctification comes through blood, not by works! So, large quantities of blood would have been poured out by Job on behalf of his seven sons and three daughters on a regular basis, but he would have also sprinkled the sacrificial blood upon each one of them!

"The Keys are in the Blood!"

It is important to remember at this point in the book that Job wasn't circumcised, he wasn't an Israelite, he wasn't part of the Blood Covenant God made with Abraham, he didn't have a Bible, and he certainly wasn't Born Again, but he was one of God's Untouchables.

"The Life is in the Blood!"

In Job 1:8 he is called "a servant". So, if the Lord

(because of the blood of sacrificed animals) would look after, protect, provide and prosper his servant Job, how much more, because of the Blood of the Lamb (and faith in that Blood), will our Heavenly Father care for his own Blood bought sons and daughters?

Also note that Job's wife, sons and daughters had no part in the sacrifice of the animals or the pouring out of their blood, Job's faith was sufficient, and a key statement in Job 1:5 is, "This Job did regularly." All that Job's wife, sons, daughters and servants had to do was to live, walk and enjoy the blessings of God that the Blood provided!

One man or woman with God, who has faith in the Blood is

"Untouchable and Unstoppable!"

Let us now move from the realm of the visible to the realm of the invisible. In Job 1:6, the veil between the two realities is parted and we are transported into a particular Realm (Dimension) of Heaven. In this particular place at a certain time, the sons of God (angels) present themselves before the Lord (the maker and owner of the Heavens and the earth (Psalm 115:15, Psalm 24:1)), and Satan is also there (because of Adam's rebellion Satan is now the delegated ruler of planet earth).

In Job 1:8 the Lord makes a powerful declaration of faith about his servant Job, then in Job 1:9 Satan makes a counter accusation, which brings us to Job 1:10.

PRAYER

"I pray that our Heavenly Father will give you the Spirit of Wisdom and Revelation concerning Job 1:10, so that the eyes of your understanding will be opened to the almighty, unstoppable power of "the Blood of Jesus", and that you will allow the eternal Holy Spirit (Hebrews 9:14) to revolutionise your life in two realities, the visible and the invisible!"

So, because of the Blood, the Lord made Job "untouchable"!

In this verse (Job 1:10) Satan (accuser) makes five statements about what the Lord (owner and maker) had done and was doing for Job, his family and all that he had. By making these five statements, Satan exposes himself and his kingdom (Ephesians 6:12) for all to see and know that there is something that he is totally powerless against, that there is something he is incapable of breaching or standing against, and this something was "the blood of the sacrifice!" In Job's case this was the regular sacrifice he made and was making on behalf of his family (Job 1:5).

"The Keys are in the Blood!"

So, let us look at statement number one.

"You have made a hedge around him!"

The source of this hedge (impenetrable defence) was the Lord, and what Satan was really saying was an accusation, "Because of you, I can't get to Job. You've put an unbreachable protection around him, that me or my kingdom (Ephesians 6:12) cannot penetrate or breach!" (In Star Trek terminology, the Lord had put a permanent force field around Job and all that he had.)

So, because of the Blood, Job was "untouchable"!

"Praying in tongues is a spiritual key that opens the door for divinely inspired thoughts and revelation about the Blood!"

Statement number two.

(Job 1:10)

"You have put a hedge" (an unbreachable protection) **"around his household."**

This means Job's wife, seven sons, three daughters and all that they had and owned were totally protected from anything Satan or his kingdom (Ephesians 6:12) was trying to send against them. Job's faith in the "blood of the sacrifice" enabled the Lord to move legally in every area of Job's life (visible and invisible) and in the lives of his family and everything he had and everything they had. John 10:10 says, "The thief comes to steal, kill and destroy." (A type of satanic bench of three.)

In Job's life (the life of his family, servants and livestock), because of his "faith in the blood", nothing was stolen, nothing died prematurely and nothing was destroyed. For Job and his family it was "days of Heaven on earth"!

Through the blood and faith in the blood, Job and his family were "untouchable"!

"The Keys are in the Blood!"

Statement number <u>three</u>.

"And around all that he has on every side."

1 Peter 5:8 says our adversary prowls around seeking

who he may devour. This is exactly what Satan was doing with Job, his family and all that he had. He was continually looking and probing for a way in to steal, kill and destroy, but Job's "faith in the blood" legally enabled Heaven to keep Hell out of his life, the life of his family and all his possessions. This must have infuriated Satan. Although he was the legal steward of planet earth, here was someone he couldn't get at or influence. Job was untouchable in the visible and the invisible.

I hope as you read this book you are beginning to see the absolute necessity of the Blood of the Lamb in your life, the life of your family, and everything you and they have. Your faith and diligent application of the Blood could revolutionise your life! The Blood of the New Covenant puts you in a place of great favour and that favour is a shield (Psalm 5:12).

"The Keys are in the Blood!"

Statement number <u>four</u>.

"You have blessed" (Proverbs 10:22) "the work of his hands."

Statement number <u>five</u>.

"And his possessions have increased in the land!"

When I read these last two accusations Satan made in Job 1:10, it is very clear to me that, because of "The Blood of the New Covenant", it has been, and always will be, our Heavenly Father's will (2 Corinthians 8:9, 1 John 5:14-15) for His Blood bought sons and daughters to prosper and be in good health, but prosperity, health, success, increase and dominion (like the new birth) are a personal choice, our Heavenly Father will never force His blessings upon us.

The Israelites in Deuteronomy 30:19 were given a choice and we, like them, must choose on a daily basis which kingdom we are going to walk in.

"The Life is in the Blood!"
"The Blood of Jesus is the Antidote for the venom of the snake and the sting of the scorpion!"

The Blood of Jesus was shed, gathered, carried and poured out on our behalf, and it is always available to sons and daughters of God, but it must be applied by faith (2 Corinthians 4:13).

So, open your mouth (Psalm 81:10) and let the Holy Spirit fill it with personal declarations about the Blood, and watch His Kingdom come and His Will being done in a new revolutionary way in your life and the life of your family!

Declaration!
In the Name of Jesus
and because of the Blood of the Lamb,
I am surrounded with the Favour of God
like a Shield!

Declaration!
Because of the Blood of the Cross,
I am one of God's Untouchables!

Declaration!
Because of the Blood of the Lamb,
I am always the head and never the tail!

Finally, I would like to state in strongest terms that we are in an **ETERNAL** Blood Covenant with God, and Jesus is the Eternal Guarantee. This means that what happened to Job, His servant, will never happen to us, His Blood bought sons and daughters, and by that I mean God will never break His own Blood Covenant of Protection and Prosperity He has made with us. (John 10:27-29, John 15:16, Hebrews 13:5c, Revelation 1:4-6)

Satan is a master of misinformation, intimidation and misdirection. Never believe the lie that God has taken His hand off you so that Satan can sift you like wheat. You are the apple of God's eye. You are washed in the Blood and all of Heaven is cheering you on. You are called today to be one of His "Untouchables".

OH THE BLOOD OF JESUS

(VERSE 3)

OH THE BLOOD OF JESUS
GIVES ME ACCESS
TO HIS THRONE OF GRACE

YES, THE BLOOD OF JESUS
CAUSES ME TO DWELL
IN THAT SECRET PLACE

OH THE PRECIOUS BLOOD
POURED OUT IN HEAVEN FOR ME

HALLELUJAH!
THE BLOOD OF JESUS HAS SET ME FREE!

4

The Untouchables: Abram/ Abraham

I would first like to start this chapter with a statement, "A blood covenant (a generational binding agreement made in blood between two parties) that does not include "protection and prosperity" is worthless!"

No father, clan leader or tribal chief would "cut the covenant" if protection and prosperity were not the two main parts of that blood agreement!

When the chief or clan leader "cut the covenant", there would be a discussion of terms, an exchange of weapons, goods and generational blessing and curses, but most important of all was "the blood"!

Abram/Abraham entered into a Blood Covenant with God (Genesis 15:7-21). Isaac, Jacob, the twelve sons and the twelve tribes all had access to the Covenant.

In today's politically correct and sanitised Christianity, the true meaning and impact of a "Blood Covenant" is all but lost. (Hosea 4:6a, "My people are destroyed, perish, and are silenced for a lack of knowledge" – Revelation.) God started with the Blood and He will finish with the Blood!

"Study the Blood!"
"The Keys are in the Blood!"

A good example of what "cutting the covenant" means can be found in Sir Henry Morton Stanley's account of his search in Africa for the Christian Pioneer and Missionary, Dr David Livingstone. (You can find this information on the Internet.)

"Get the Blood to the Body!"

The account of Abram's life starts in Genesis 11:27. Abram (high father), his wife Sarah (dominative), his father Terah (delay, wanderer), his brother, uncles, aunts and all his relatives were born, raised and lived in Ur of the Chaldean. (Chaldean can mean astrology and the Chaldean raiders were the ones who stole Job's three thousand camels and killed his servants with the edge of the sword, Job 1:17.)

Terah, Abram and all the inhabitants of Ur and throughout Chaldean were moon and star worshippers and they served other Gods (Joshua 24:2). This meant that astrology was a dominant and powerful force and influence in their daily lives and throughout the nation of Chaldea. So various offerings would have been made by Terah, Abram and their families at the local altars and in the main temples (including blood sacrifices). This would have been done on a regular basis. Their basic theology was, "If we can keep the gods happy, then maybe they will bless, protect and prosper us."

This type of religious thinking originated from the Tree of the Knowledge of Good and Evil (Genesis 2:17) and all it produces is fear, works, disappointment, anger and death. Sadly after 2000 years of a new Blood Covenant with Jesus as the guarantee (Hebrews 7:22), so many of God's people still have the same type of mind set, fear, works and disappointment, hoping to keep God happy by what they are not doing and by what they are doing, and if possible make it through their lives and eventually get into Heaven, but there is no dominion in their lives! This is not what Jesus shed His Blood for! Like Abram, we, the people of God, need a serious mind change (Romans 12:2). On our side of the cross, we need a divine Blood Transfusion!

Question: How did God change Abram's mind?

Firstly, let us look at "Saul the Pharisee" and "Peter the Apostle". Both these men needed radical mindset changes, both were trapped in generational religious bondage. If we don't allow the Holy Spirit the freedom to deal with ungodly generational belief systems in our souls, in our bodies (fallen DNA), then the old mindsets and ungodly desires will continue to rise to the surface of our minds and emotions and try to deceive us and lead us astray (steal, kill, destroy).

"The Blood of Jesus is the Antidote for the venom of the snake and the sting of the scorpion!"

Saul the Pharisee

Saul was a man on a mission. His mission was to imprison, kill and destroy (John 10:10a) as many of the followers of the Way as he could. (Saul was Satan's main man at that time.) Basically he was a murderer, religious bigot, full of hate and self righteousness. He had to be stopped, and I believe that the Ecclesia had two prayer options.

1. Lord, save him, or
2. Lord, remove him!

In Acts 9 we have the account of Saul's radical conversion experience and total mind renewal. The King of kings appeared to him personally on the road to Damascus and says, "Saul, why are you persecuting me?" Saul's reply was, "Who are you Lord?" (Remember, ignorance is our enemy.) The reply from the King of kings was, "I am Jesus!" Those three words totally transformed Saul's life, renewed his mind, set him free from generational religious bondage and put him on a path that he would never have chosen for himself. It took a powerful encounter with the King of kings and the Rhema Word, "I AM JESUS!" to completely revolutionise Saul's life and move him out of the Law and into a "New Blood Covenant"!

"The Keys are in the Blood!"

Peter the Apostle

In Acts 10:10, Jesus, the King of kings has a special mission lined up for his Ambassador, Peter, but in order for Peter to fulfil that mission, he was going to have to experience a radical mindset change!

His mission was to go to the house of a Roman

Centurion and to present to him, his family and household, the Gospel (Good News) of Jesus Christ!

This was mission impossible for Peter, because even after the phenomenal event of Pentecost, there was still a generational, religious, racist stronghold in his soul/mind. (Cornelius was a gentile, and as far as the Jews were concerned, they were unclean and worse than dogs.) So, for Peter, the generational issues were an invisible, impenetrable wall that he would not be able to get through himself. So, like Saul, God stepped in (Acts 10:9-16). Peter is on the roof, he's hungry and he falls into an "Extasis" – Ecstacy – Trance. Heaven is open! Peter is told to eat unclean animals, unclean birds and creeping things. Peter's answer is, "No!" (This is an amazing reply! Read Acts 2 through to Acts 6 and see how Peter was being used to advance the Kingdom, yet he said, "No" to God.) So the soul releasing, mind renewing Rhema Word came to Peter, **"What God has cleansed you must not call unclean!"**

Peter is now free to step into the next part of his mission (Acts 10:17-48). Also, he received the boldness to stand before the other Apostles and Jewish believers in Jerusalem and testify to what had happened.

"The Life is in the Blood!"

So, how did God release Abram from generations of astrological idolatry?

The answer is very simple! "He showed him the stars" (Genesis 15:5) and then released the Rhema Word, "So shall your seed be." There is a statement in Genesis 15:6 and it says, "And he (Abram) believed in the Lord." That was the moment when Abram's soul was delivered. He left the road of paganism and idolatry, and he started his journey as a patriarch and a man of faith! The Rhema Word is the "Sword of the Spirit!" (Ephesians 6:17b) and nothing from Abram's generational past, Saul's past, Peter's past or our past can resist the Rhema Word of God (Psalm 107:20, Matthew 4:4).

"The Life is in the Blood!"
"Study the Blood!"
"The Keys are in the Blood!"
"Get the Blood to the Body!"
"Walk through the Realms of My Blood!"

Every blood covenant must have two main components, protection and prosperity, incorporated into the terms of that blood agreement. All humans throughout the ages, no matter what nation or culture, right up to the present time and beyond (individually or collectively), want to be safe, secure (protection) and successful (prosperity). These two blood covenant principles are stated very clearly by God to Abram. (Before blood is shed, a blood agreement is entered into, the terms are discussed and declared by the two parties.) In Genesis 15:1, the Lord says, "Do not be afraid Abram, I am your shield" (protection). God didn't say I will give you a shield, He said, "I am your shield!" In blood covenant language, the Lord was saying, "Abram, I will personally stand between you and all your enemies, natural and supernatural, visible and invisible, and if necessary, I will give my life for yours!"

What an amazing Blood Covenant statement! Abram has now become one of the "untouchables"!

Then God said, "I am your extremely great reward" (prosperity). This means ongoing, continuous increased prosperity, wealth and riches beyond what his (Abraham) natural mind could grasp or conceive (Ephesians 3:20). It was for Abram throughout his life on earth (175 years). Abram did not need the benefits of a blood covenant (protection and prosperity) after he died, he needed them while he was alive on earth and so do we!

"Study the Blood of the New Covenant!" *"The Keys are in the Blood!"*

Finally, let us look at a couple of statements in Galatians 3:

"Therefore know that only those who are of faith are sons of Abraham!"

"So then those who are of faith are blessed with believing Abraham!"

"Christ redeemed us from the curse of the Law, that the blessings of Abraham might come upon the Gentiles in Christ Jesus, that we might receive the promise of the Spirit through faith!"

"If you are Christ's, then you are Abraham's seed and heirs according to the Promise!"

The moment we ask Jesus into our lives, we enter into a new and better Blood Covenant with Jesus as our guarantee. This means that all oaths, promises and blessings that God gave Abram/Abraham are ours in Christ, if we confess with our mouth (Romans 10:10) what we believe in our hearts about the Blood, and if we speak what we believe (2 Corinthians 4:13) about the Blood, then the Holy Spirit and the Angels will manifest the protection and prosperity which is ours in Christ through the Blood Covenant!

Declarations!

I declare that, because of the Blood of Jesus,
the world cannot hold me!

I declare that, because of the Blood of Jesus,
the devil cannot stop me!

I declare that, because of the Blood of Jesus,
the past cannot restrain me!

I declare that, because of the Blood of Jesus,
time and space cannot contain me!

I declare that, because of the Blood of Jesus,
"As He is, so am I in this world!"

I declare that, because of the Blood of Jesus,
I am one of God's "Untouchables"!
"The Blood avails for me!"

OH THE BLOOD OF JESUS

(VERSE 4)

OH THE BLOOD OF JESUS
BRINGS HEALING HERE TO EARTH

YES THE BLOOD OF JESUS
IS THE LIFE OF THE NEW BIRTH

OH THE PRECIOUS BLOOD
APPLIED BY THE HOLY SPIRIT

HALLELUJAH!
THE BLOOD OF JESUS
ITS POWER KNOWS NO LIMIT!

5

The Untouchables: Moses and the Israelites

The nation of Israel had been in Egypt (Goshen) for about four hundred years. Goshen had been given to Jacob, his son Joseph and his brothers, by Pharaoh. (Genesis 47:5-6) During that four hundred year period the Israelite population had flourished to the point where the Egyptian leaders were extremely afraid of them and their increasing numbers. (Exodus 1:8-12, Psalm 105:24) By the time Moses was called and commissioned by God (Exodus 3 and 4), the Israelites were suffering and under great oppression. The call on Moses' life was basically to deliver God's people out of Egypt and lead them into the land God had promised Abram through and by the Blood

Covenant (Genesis 15:18), but God also had a bigger plan and that was to judge and humiliate in two realities (the visible and the invisible), the principalities, thrones, power and elemental spirits the Egyptians worshipped (Exodus 12:12). This was going to be just a small foretaste of what was going to happen when "The Word became flesh" (John 1:14), and completely and utterly "destroyed the works of the devil" (1 John 3:8b) and made a "public spectacle of them" (Colossians 2:15), through and by "The Blood of the Cross"! So, since the resurrection two thousand years ago, any man or woman can enter into the "New Blood Covenant" with Jesus as the guarantee (Hebrews 7:22), through and by faith, and experience what is called "the new birth"!

"Remember, the two essential components of a Blood Covenant are Protection and Prosperity!"

After Moses' first encounter with Pharaoh, life got increasingly worse for the Israelites (Exodus 5:1-21) to the point where they wouldn't even listen to what God had to say through Moses (Exodus 6:9). So, this brings us to Exodus 7:14-25.

"When the waters became blood!"

The River Nile and the waters of Egypt were God's first target for a national/public display of His power.

Pharaoh, the Egyptians and the Israelites were going to see and experience something that had never happened before!

(The River Nile is approximately 4,000 miles long. It is formed by three other rivers; the Blue Nile, the Black Nile and the White Nile, all converging together at a place we know as Khartoum! 79.2 billion gallons of water flow down the Nile on a daily basis as it journeys to the Mediterranean Sea. The Nile is said to be the longest river in the World.)

"Study the Blood!"

Every morning Pharaoh would leave his palace and go down to the Nile (Exodus 7:15b), not to wash, but to engage with the demon spirit of the Nile. The River Nile to the Egyptians was their life source, and the demonic prince/power of the Nile that they worshipped was called "Hapi". Water spirits or river spirits are real, and when Pharaoh daily engaged with the water spirit of the Nile, he received power. (When the Blood Covenant believers engage with the Holy Spirit, they also are supposed to receive power, Luke 24:49, Acts 2:8, Ephesians 5:18b.)

At this point, I would like to give testimony (Revelation 12:11) of deliverance from a water spirit. (The person's name will not be given, only her initials.) When CLB came to us (2017), she was on a heavy medication programme of morphine for pain management (without going into detail, the Holy Spirit set her free). Then one night at a meeting she came and told me that she had just seen in a vision "a snake swimming towards her under the water". I told her, from my experience (testimony), that it was a "water spirit", something that she had not heard of before (the kingdom of darkness works on and in our ignorance). This made complete sense to her because she had been experiencing strange occurrences with water in her car and in her house. On a regular basis, on dry days, water would appear in her car. After trying to find the cause (many times), she took the car to the garage where the mechanics stripped the car down to see if they could find the source of the water. They didn't because the source of the water wasn't natural. Also, on dry days, water would rise up through the floor of her kitchen causing her to have her kitchen completely removed. This happened three times! (This particular lady had strong generational connections to freemasons, and freemasonry is satanism with a respectable face.) So, in the meeting that night she received prayer (in the Name of Jesus) and the situation was resolved!

"The Life is in the Blood!"

So let us continue with Moses, Aaron and Pharaoh. Moses was told to meet Pharaoh on the banks of the Nile and tell him "To let God's people go." Pharaoh refused. Moses was told to strike the waters of the Nile with his rod and it would turn into blood. Aaron was told to stretch out his rod over the land of Egypt and all the water (rivers, streams, pools, ponds and water that was stored) would also turn to blood! They did as they were commanded by God, and the Nile and all the waters of Egypt were "Turned to blood, the fish died, the river stank and the Egyptians couldn't drink!" This lasted seven days (Exodus 7:16-25). So, over a seven day period, approximately 524 billion gallons of blood flowed down the Nile, and all the land that would be normally irrigated by water of the Nile was now being soaked in blood! So, because of Moses and Aaron's fearless obedience (which made them untouchable), the land of Egypt was covered in blood! This for the Egyptians was a national disaster, because this blood brought nothing but drought and death. For the god of the Nile, Hapi, he/it was defeated, dethroned and humiliated!

"The Keys are in the Blood!"

Let us quickly look at the account of the "waters becoming blood" from our side of the Cross. Today we need in our towns, cities, villages and regions, exactly what happened in Egypt to the Egyptians, but (in a Kingdom or Heavenly context) we need a tsunami of the Blood of Jesus to flood our cities and regions. Every man, woman and child in our towns and cities needs to be soaked, deluged and drenched in the Blood of the Lamb. The Blood of the Lamb is the legal basis of everything God does on Planet Earth. So, in order to fulfil "The Great Commission", the Ecclesia must have a fresh revelation and experience of the mighty power of the Blood of Jesus!

"No Blood, No Fire!"

Let us now move quickly through plagues two and three.

Number two was a plague of frogs (Exodus 8:1-15). Heket (woman's body with a frog's head) was the goddess the Egyptians worshipped and, in this encounter, she/it was totally defeated, dethroned and humiliated!

The third plague was lice (Exodus 8:16-19). Get was the Egyptian god of the dust of the earth. He/it was also totally defeated, dethroned and humiliated!

This now brings us to plague number four. This plague has significant implications for us today. The fourth plague was a plague of flies (Exodus 8:20-32). Khepri (a man with a fly's head) was the god the Egyptians worshipped.

God tells Pharaoh, through Moses, that He will send "swarms of flies" into Egypt and the houses of Egypt unless he "Lets His people go!" The difference with this plague is that there will be "no flies" in the land of Goshen. (Because of the Blood the blessings of Goshen are ours today in Jesus' Name.) This is exactly what happened. Pharaoh's house and the houses of his servants and all the land of Egypt are filled with "thick swarms of flies", and because of this, "the land is corrupted!"

There were "no flies in Goshen", so, once again, in this fourth power encounter, another Egyptian god was defeated, dethroned and humiliated!

(I believe that at this point Satan and his kingdom (Ephesians 6:12) are starting to panic. He is watching the systematic dissection of a superpower that he initiated and controlled and there was nothing he could do about it!)

"Study the Blood!"

Let us now look at the implications of this political "Power Encounter" (plague number four) in our own lives. In Luke 11:15 Jesus is accused (Revelation 12:10) (Satan is the accuser) of casting out demons by Beelzebub/Beelzebul, the ruler of demons. This name can be translated "lord of the flies" (2 Kings 1:1-4). So, there are two inter realm connections here between "visible flies that live in and on filth", and invisible demons that live in and on filth! As Blood bought sons and daughters we can, by faith in the Blood of the New Covenant, expect our King to do for us (expectation prepares the way for manifestation) what He did for Job (Job 1:1-10), Abram (Genesis 15:1), and the Israelites in Goshen (Exodus 8:22-23). Total and complete protection! It is possible by faith in the Blood to live a life in a demon free zone.

"Study the Blood!"
"The Keys are in the Blood!"

So, the thick swarms of flies could not enter Goshen, because God had made a distinction between his people and the Egyptians. That same protection and distinction is ours today through faith in the Blood of the Cross, the Blood of Jesus Christ, the Blood of the Lamb, and the Blood of the New Covenant.

Demons have no right to the soul, mind, body or life of Blood bought sons and daughters of God!

The New Blood Covenant that we are in is better (Hebrews 7:22) than all the Old Testament blood covenants put together, but we must mix the eternal Word of God about the Blood with faith (Hebrews 4:2c) and declare (2 Corinthians 4:13, 18) what the Blood of Jesus, the Blood of the Cross, the Blood of the Lamb and the Blood of the New Covenant has done and is doing for us (Proverbs 18:22)!

Holy Spirit inspired declarations about the Blood will revolutionise the life of God's people, internally and externally, in the visible and the invisible!

Declarations!

I declare, in the Name of Jesus
and because of the Blood of the Lamb,
I am the righteousness of God in Christ!

I declare, in the Name of Jesus
and because of the Blood of the Cross,
no weapon formed against me,
past, present or future, can prosper!

I declare, in the Name of Jesus
and because of the Blood of Jesus,
as He is, so I am in this world, "untouchable"!

"The Life is in the Blood!"

We are through and by the Blood of Jesus eternally redeemed (Ephesians 1:7), eternally righteous (Romans 5:9), eternally sanctified (Hebrews 13:12), and eternally glorified (Romans 8:30). None of this is through any works of our own (Ephesians 2:5), it's all through the amazing gift of God's love and grace!

So let us choose to live by faith in "the blessings of Goshen", to live, move and prosper in "demon free zones", and to walk out our lives here on earth in Heaven's transfiguring power (Isaiah 60:1, 2a, 3)

"There is power, power,
wonder working power,
In the Blood of the Lamb!"

Power encounter number five (Exodus 9:1-7) and once again Moses told Pharaoh, "Let My people go", and once again Pharaoh refused. This time the Egyptian livestock (cattle, horses, donkeys, camels, oxen and sheep) were going to suffer a severe pestilence (Exodus 9:3). "Hathor" was the demon/ spirit that the Egyptians worshipped and looked to for protection (it had the body of a woman and the head of a cow). In Exodus 9:4-7 we see once again "protection" in Goshen and "a distinction" between the livestock of the Israelites and the Egyptians. "No pestilence in Goshen!" "No death in Goshen!" Hathor is totally defeated, dethroned and humiliated!

Plague number six, "boils" (Exodus 9:8-12). This (demon/spirit) was the Egyptian goddess of medicine, Isis, so when the plague of boils came upon the Egyptians and the magicians (Exodus 9:11), there was nothing she/it could do to stop it. Once again another false god (demon) defeated, dethroned and humiliated!

Plague number seven, "hail" (Exodus 9:18-35). The hail came down upon Egypt in great destructive power (Exodus 9:23-25), but in Goshen there was "no hail"! Nut was the Egyptian goddess of the sky, and she/it was totally defeated, dethroned and humiliated!

"There is no God like our God!"
"The Life is in the Blood!"
"Study the Blood!"

Plague number eight, "locusts" (Exodus 10:3-20). Seth was the Egyptian God (demon/spirit) looked to for protection by the Egyptians during the plague. He/it had the body of a man and the head of an animal. Seth was powerless. The locusts came and he/it was defeated, dethroned and humiliated!

"What a mighty God we serve!"

Eight demon powers defeated, only two more to go!

Plague number nine, "darkness" (Exodus 10:21-29). Once again we see a distinction between the land of Goshen and the land of Egypt. In Egypt the darkness was so intense and oppressive that the Egyptians could not even leave their houses (three days), but in Goshen, "All the children of Israel had light in their homes"! As far as Ra (sun god) was concerned, he/it was defeated, dethroned and humiliated! No contest! Hallelujah!

"Jesus is the light of the World and
through the Blood of the New Covenant
the blessings of Goshen are ours!
(Distinction and Protection)"

"Study the Blood!"

Moses in Exodus 12:21 called the elders (fathers) of Israel and told them to, "Pick out and take lambs for yourselves according to your families (a lamb's blood for a family) and kill the lamb." Moses did not need to tell them how to kill the lamb or where to kill the lamb. Every father understood what needed to be done. It was part of their culture and it was part of Egyptian culture. Blood sacrifice and honouring people with blood was a regular part of life in the times of the Israelites in Egypt and in other nations.

The lamb had to have its throat cut and its blood drained into a basin, which was a depression in the threshold of the house (not a basin you picked up and carried outside). This is known as the threshold covenant. The reason being that the threshold of a house was a very important and sacred place, because whoever the father of the house allowed to step over the blood of the sacrifice, which had been poured out on the threshold, and enter the house, this signified a blood agreement with the visitor, his lifestyle and his gods. The threshold was very important! (1 Samuel 5:4-5, Zephaniah 1:9, Hebrews 10:29, 2 John 1:10)

Depending on the importance of the visitor dictated the selection of the animal to be bled and sacrificed. The more important the visitor, the more expensive and valuable the sacrifice! (John 1:29, 36)

"Study the Blood!"

So the lamb had its throat cut, all of its blood was poured out into the basin in the threshold. The lamb was then taken into the house and was roasted and eaten by everyone in the house. As important as all these instructions and events were, none of them could protect the Israelites' first born from the plague and death that was to come (John 10:10b).

The most important part of this divine strategy was "The application of the blood." (Exodus 12:22-23)

It was the "Blood of the Lamb" (Revelation 12:11a) applied by the father of the house that would stop the plague and the spirit of death (John 10:10b) from crossing the threshold, entering the house and killing the first born!

God was very specific (through Moses) on how the blood was to be applied and where the blood was to be applied (Exodus 12:22), "With hyssop strike the lintel and the doorposts with the blood."

(The hyssop plant was used by the Egyptian priests for religious purification.)

So, as the father applied the blood of the lamb to the lintel and the doorposts, the blood would also be splattered (1 Peter 1:25) on his hands, on his arms, it would be on his head, his clothes and his beard, now the whole entrance to his house is covered in lamb's blood, the last thing he had to do was to step over the threshold and go through the door (John 10:9a), which was dripping in lamb's blood!

"Study the Blood!"
"The Life is in the Blood!"
"The Keys are in the Blood!"

Now for the father and his household, it was just a matter of eating the roasted lamb and waiting (by faith) to see what was going to happen!

When midnight came, death came, and every house where there was no blood in the basin (threshold) or on the lintel and doorposts, death stepped over the threshold into the house and killed the firstborn, but because of the blood of the lamb, the Israelites were "protected" (Psalm 91:5-10).

"You shall not be afraid of the terror by night,
Nor of the pestilence that walks in darkness.
A thousand may fall at your side,
And ten thousand at your right hand;
But it shall not come near you.
Only with your eyes shall you look,
And see the reward of the wicked.
No evil shall befall you,
Nor shall any plague come near your dwelling."

Psalm 91 is a Blood Covenant Psalm, "Protection and Prosperity."

Now would be a good place to make this statement, "Death needs a door!"

In the Garden of Eden when Eve was deceived by Satan and ate the forbidden fruit from the Tree of the Knowledge of Good and Evil, nothing changed, everything remained the same, "perfect", but when Adam ate the fruit, everything changed instantly. Sin and death entered his blood, his DNA was changed, he died spiritually (separation from God), and after 930 years, he died physically. Adam was the door by which sin and death entered the human race, and all life on planet earth!

Every man, woman and child is a blood relative of Adam.

Human blood carried the sentence of death within it. Human blood is "poisoned" and the hereditary blood poisoning (sin) always results in death, unless God intervenes and this is what He did for Enoch and Elijah!

"Faith in the Blood of the Lamb
and the application of the Blood of the Lamb
is the key which locks the doors
to sickness, poverty and death!"

In Israel, the fathers of the house had to apply the blood. Today the father must apply the Blood (Malachi 4:6a, Hosea 13:14a and 14b, Zechariah 9:11), born again, biological fathers, spiritual fathers, city fathers, regional fathers and national fathers!

Every man is a door, and for those of us who are born again, applying the "Blood of the Lamb by faith" is to keep sickness, poverty and death outside the house!

I would now like to share a testimony I was given on applying the Blood of the Lamb by faith.

Testimony (Revelation 12:11)

(The person's name will not be given, only his initials.)

LA "I was born again in 1993. Soon after, the Holy Spirit led me to Paul and Linda Fenwick. Over the years, Paul has taught on "the Blood" many times. The Bible states that God creates everything through and by His Word! One of the things I was told in the early days, was that we could cover people (by faith) in the Blood of Jesus! The Holy Spirit gave me a revelation of this and He led me to apply this to my family.

My younger brother had started taking heavy drugs from his early twenties, for over a decade. Regularly, I would verbally (by faith) cover my brother in the Blood of Jesus, trusting for his deliverance! As the years went by, I would find out that people he knew, who were also on heavy drugs, had died. However, twenty-seven years later (2021), my brother is still alive, born again and is no longer taking drugs!

Faith in the Blood and the verbal application (2 Corinthians 4:13) of the Blood always gets results.

Job 22:30, "He will deliver one who is not innocent, Yes he will be delivered by the purity (by the Blood) of your hands."

"No Blood, No Fire!"

Let us return to the Israelites in Egypt. The plague had descended, death had reaped a harvest among the Egyptian first born, but in Goshen death could not pass through the blood and not one Israelite first born died! Pharaoh's reaction was to tell Moses and Aaron to "Get out of Egypt" and also the Israelites, their children and their livestock (Exodus 12:31-33).

"Study the Blood!"

In Chapter Four of this book, I made the statement that every blood covenant that was worth anything had to have the two main components of "PROTECTION and PROSPERITY" in it (Genesis 15:1). Throughout the ten plagues in Egypt we see God's Blood Covenant Promise (oath) of "protection" in Goshen in full operation.

1. No flies!
2. No darkness!
3. No death!

Now in Exodus 12:35-36 we see the second plan of God's Blood Covenant Promise (oath) of "prosperity", because of the favour which God put on the Israelites (Exodus 12:36). The Egyptians handed over their gold, silver (Job 27:16-17; Proverbs 13:22b) and clothing. It says in Exodus 12:36c, "Thus they (Israelites) plundered the Egyptians." In verses 41 and 51 it states that, when the Israelites left Egypt, they didn't stagger or limp out, they left "according to their armies"

David, the Warrior King and Prophet, while in the spirit, describes the event in Psalm 105:37 and 43:

"He also brought them out with silver and gold. There was none feeble (kaw-shal – weak, faint) among his tribes!"

"He brought out his people with joy (saw-sone – gladness and rejoicing)!"

Ephesians 6:10, "Finally, be strong in the Lord and in the power of His might!"

After Moses and the Israelites marched out of Egypt carrying Egyptian gold, silver, clothes and resources, they miraculously crossed the Red Sea (on dry ground), headed towards the River Jordan and the promised land, there is an event concerning the Blood, which is recorded in Exodus 24:4-8 and also in Hebrews 9:19-20.

Moses rose early (Exodus 24:4) and built an altar at the base of Mount Sinai, the reason for this was "sanctification". On that day there was going to be multiple sacrifices of oxen, Yahweh wanted all the people of Israel (two million) men, women and children, covered in blood. In order to soak the altar and cover two million people with blood, it would require many, many oxen. It would mean that Moses would have to kill a strong, healthy ox, immobilise it, cut its throat and drain all the blood (ten gallons) into basins/containers, then cut the dead animal into pieces and place it on the altar! For Moses to do this once would have been extremely strenuous, but to have to do it again and again and again throughout the day would have been beyond his physical ability. In Exodus 24:5, it says that the young men of Israel were also recruited for this monumental, bloody task! The account in Exodus and Hebrews are very brief, but if you can use your sanctified imagination regarding this national event, you will hear the bellowing of the oxen as they are being slaughtered, the ever increasing smell of blood as it is poured into basin after basin, then the cutting up of the dead animals, plus two million men, women and children standing watching and waiting! By the time all the basins/containers were brim full of blood, Moses, Aaron and all the young men would have been totally covered from head to toe in blood. It must have been a wild sight to see!

In Exodus 24:6, it says that Moses took half the total amount of blood (about ten gallons per ox, which could have amounted to more than 100 gallons of blood), and poured it all over the altar. The altar and the ground around the altar would have been drenched and soaked in blood (all this is a shadow of the Blood of Jesus). Then it says in Hebrews 9:19 that he took the blood and sprinkled it on the Book!

The Bible that you read or meditate on is a Blood-sprinkled Book. Only a Blood-sprinkled Book could withstand all Hells efforts to suppress it and remove it from the Earth! Only a Blood-sprinkled Book could maintain its Heavenly power! Only a Blood-sprinkled Book can ignite hope in our hearts! After sprinkling the Book, all the Israelites (two million) were sprinkled with blood. This was a national sanctification programme commanded by Yahweh. It is a shadow of what happens to any individual when they give their lives to Jesus, they are washed in the Blood of the Sacrifice (the Lamb of God). The ox blood that the Israelites were sprinkled with would soon dry out, but the Blood of the Lamb is eternally alive, eternally fresh and it never loses its life giving power!

Protection and prosperity is yours through faith in the Blood of Jesus!

OH THE BLOOD OF JESUS

(VERSE 5)

OH THE BLOOD OF JESUS
SHED ON THE CROSS FOR ME

YES, THE BLOOD OF JESUS
SHED ON CALVARY'S TREE

OH, THE BLOOD OF JESUS
POURED OUT ON THE MERCY SEAT ABOVE

HALLELUJAH!
FOR THE BLOOD OF JESUS
THE FATHER'S PERFECT GIFT OF LOVE!

6

The Untouchables: Rahab and David

RAHAB

The account of Rahab (her name means proud or haughty) and her family's protection and deliverance from Jericho is a tremendous testimony of God's "Amazing Grace"! (Joshua 2, 6:22-25)

Joshua commissioned two spies and sent them across the Jordan on a reconnaissance mission (a military observation of a region or place to locate the enemy and ascertain strategic information and feature). The target was Jericho! (Jericho was a Canaanite city.)

The two spies that Joshua sent out were very brave

men, they didn't stay outside the city and observe from a distance or a safe place, but they went right into Jericho itself! They were seen and recognised (Joshua 2:2). This caused a city-wide manhunt to be put into operation by the king, his soldiers and the people of Jericho. When night came, the city gate was shut and Jericho went into "lockdown", fear being the motivating force!

Question: Where do two male Israelite spies go to hide (in plain sight) in a hostile Canaanite city?

The answer is simple! In a brothel, in what we would call the "red light" area of the city (Joshua 2:1c).

Rahab's house would have been a well known location to all the male travellers, strangers and merchants going to and from Jericho. When the king of Jericho questioned Rahab about the location of the two spies, she lied to him and misdirected him (Joshua 2:3-7).

In Joshua 2:9-11, Rahab declares to the two spies that she and the whole city of Jericho know that, "The Lord has given them the land and how forty years earlier God parted the Red Sea and also what they did to Sihon, king of the Amorites (Numbers 21:21-24), and to Og the giant king of Bashan (Deuteronomy

3:3, 11)." In Joshua 2:9, 11, Rahab gives them a report on the mental and emotional condition of the king, the army and the civil population of Jericho. They were in terror, their hearts had melted and their courage had gone!

Let us now go back in time to Numbers 14:9, forty years before Rahab and the two spies. In this account in Numbers 14:9, Joshua makes an amazing statement by the Holy Spirit, the veil between the visible and the invisible has been parted and he is allowed to see something which the other spies couldn't see. Joshua speaks up and prophetically declares about the nations which they had been spying upon that "Their protection has departed from them!" This is an amazing statement because the walls of Jericho were standing strong and wouldn't collapse for another forty years and the cities of the giants were heavily fortified! So the question is, "What was he talking about and what protection had gone?"

The answer to this question has great significance for the blood bought sons and daughters of God today!

Firstly, let us look at the word "protection". The Hebrew word is "tsale", it means "shade" or "defence". The root word is "tsaw-lal", which means "hovering". So in the visible realm, Jericho's protection was its walls, but in the invisible realm,

Jericho's protection/defence covering was a demonic prince and a host of wicked spirits (Ephesians 6:12) which were ruling, reigning and directing all levels of life in Jericho. This means that forty years before the Walls of Jericho came down, God had already defeated, dethroned, humiliated and evicted the demonic prince and powers from Jericho.

The Israelites wasted forty years in the wilderness because they chose to listen and believe fake news from their frightened leaders (Numbers 14:27-37).

Fear is:

F alse
E vidence
A ppearing
R eal

They could have boldly marched straight into the promised land (by faith) on the strength of the "blood covenant" God made with Abram in Genesis 15:1!

"DO NOT BE AFRAID,
I AM YOUR SHIELD,
YOUR EXCEEDINGLY GREAT REWARD!"

"Study the Blood!"

So what God did for the Israelites in Joshua's day (He gave them an open heaven), Jesus has done for us in our day. Our King has totally and eternally defeated, dethroned, stripped, disarmed and humiliated Satan and his government (Ephesians 6:12).

(Matthew 28:18) Jesus came and said, "All authority has been given to me in heaven and on earth!"

(Colossians 2:15) By going to the cross and being raised from the dead on the third day, He disarmed principalities and powers, he made a public spectacle (humiliated) of them, triumphing (totally victorious) over them in it (the cross)!

(Ephesians 1:20-23) How God "Raised Jesus from the dead and seated Him (us) at His right hand in the heavenly places, far above all principality, power, might and dominion, and every name that is named, not only in this age but also in that which is to come, and God put all things under His feet!"

(Philippians 2:9-11) "Therefore God has highly exalted (raised to the highest position) Him and has given Him the name (position, authority and character) which is above every name, that at the name (position, authority and character) of Jesus every knee should bow, in heaven, on earth and under the earth and <u>every</u> tongue confess that Jesus Christ is Lord!"

(1 John 3:8b) "For this purpose (original intent), the Son of God was manifested, that He might destroy the works (acts, deeds and labours) of the devil!"

The five scriptures quoted tell us exactly what Jesus our King has done, so let us choose to walk by faith on a daily basis in the total and fully completed work of the Cross!

"Study the Blood!"
"The Life is in the Blood!"
"The Keys are in the Blood!"

Let us now return to Rahab (proud and haughty) and the two (the number of agreement) spies.

Jericho was a Canaanite city and in Deuteronomy 20:17-18, the Word of the Lord through Moses to the Israelite Army about Jericho was very clear, they were to utterly destroy everything; men, women, children and livestock. Then they were to burn all the bodies and city with fire! (Joshua 6:24a) This may seem like serious overkill, but Jericho had at least 20,000 inhabitants, plus all their livestock. If the bodies had been left to rot, maggots, flies and spreading diseases would have been the end result. Burning the city and the bodies stopped any pestilence or disease coming out or spreading from the ruins of Jericho! (Genesis 19:24) "Fire cleanses!" (Isaiah 6:6-7) (Acts 2:3)

So, as we can see very clearly, the Word of the Lord (through Moses) was "No prisoners, no survivors!" The salvation of Rahab and her family was miraculous, because it went against God's original command!

Question: Why was this allowed?

"Study the Blood!"

Rahab, by hiding the spies (Joshua 2:6), lying and misdirecting the king of Jericho, put herself in a place of great favour with the two spies, who were also in a "blood covenant" (through circumcision) with Almighty God! They were now in her debt. They owed her their lives, and through her actions, the God of Abraham, Isaac and Jacob was also in her debt. (Rahab, despite her profession, was a very clever, wise and shrewd woman.) So, Yahweh (because of the blood covenant, "I will bless those who bless you") had to reciprocate! So, through the spies, Yahweh released a strategy (the correct approach in achieving the desired targeted purpose) (Joshua 2:14, 18). God's love, grace, mercy, kindness, favour and forgiveness far outweighs his judgement.

Everything changes when “the blood” is involved. Yahweh was not only going to save and deliver Rahab, but also as many people who would listen to her and enter her house when the Israelite Army attacked. Rahab let the spies escape through a window in her house and told them what to do in order to get back to the Israelite Camp safely. Their reply to her was, “Bind a scarlet cord from your window.” (Joshua 2:18) This represented “the blood” and would give Rahab and her family (if they listened to the instructions) complete protection. They would become

“UNTOUCHABLE!”

“Study the Blood!”
“The Keys are in the Blood!”

The grace of God is amazing! His forgiveness, mercy, kindness and favour are beyond our comprehension. The truth about “the blood” in the life of Job and Rahab are signposts and keys for our lives today! Job and Rahab were two very different people. Their lifestyles were different. Their families were different. Their occupations were different. Job was an Uzzite and Rahab was a Canaanite, but “the blood” is no respecter of gender, age, culture or nationality. Today, the Blood of the Lamb is available to all who will call on the name (position, authority, character) of the Lord!

"Study the Blood!"

Let us briefly compare Job with Rahab.

1. Job was blameless	– Rahab was guilty
2. Job was righteous	– Rahab was unrighteous
3. Job feared God	– Rahab was a Canaanite and she worshipped demons
4. Job shunned evil	– Rahab had embraced it all her life

Job's good qualities and Rahab's bad qualities were irrelevant where the blood was concerned. It is "faith in the blood" not works that "PROTECTS AND PROSPERS"!

Rahab did as she was instructed and in Joshua 6:22-25 we see the outcome of her faith. Rahab, her father and mother, brothers (no mention of sisters), all that she had and all her relatives were "protected and delivered"! Satan cannot withstand the blood or break through the protecting power of the blood and not only that, Rahab is eternally honoured in Matthew's account of the Genealogy of Jesus Christ (Matthew 1:5).

So, like Job and his family, Abram, Isaac and Jacob, the Israelites in Goshen and the Israelite first born, Rahab and her father and relatives, because of the blood, moved into the ranks of the "Untouchables"!

Before we move on to David, I would like to end this section with this statement, "If you are Born Again, you cannot improve on what the Blood of Jesus has done for you. Turn your back on a work based church life and Christianity and step forward into your heavenly destiny (Psalm 139:16). As a Blood bought, Blood washed, totally forgiven (past, present and future) son/daughter of the living God, you are in a "New Blood Covenant" with Jesus (the King of kings) as your "guarantee"! Protection and prosperity are your continuous Blood Covenant rights as you walk out your journey here on earth!

"Study the Blood!"
"The Life is in the Blood!"
"The Keys are in the Blood!"

"As He is, so are we in this world!"

"You are eternally righteous through The Blood of Jesus!"

"The Blood of Jesus is the Antidote
for the venom of the snake (Satan/demons)
and the sting of the scorpion (death)!"

"The Rhema Word of God
Given to the Sons and Daughters of God
By the Spirit of God
About the Blood of God
Clears the Way for the Manifestation of God!"

DAVID

David was and is a well known historical figure in the church and in the world. His high profile comes from killing Goliath when he was a young man and his affair with Bathsheba when he was king. There has been a number of movies about "David and Goliath" and "David and Bathsheba", but our focus is on "DAVID THE UNTOUCHABLE!"

It is possible that David was illegitimate.

In Psalm 22:9-10 he says,
"You are He who took Me out of the womb;
You made Me trust while on My mother's breasts.
I was cast (thrown) upon You from birth.
From My mother's womb You have been My God."

Psalm 51:5, David says,
"I was brought forth in iniquity,
And in sin my mother conceived me."

It seems David's childhood and teenage years were very unpleasant.

Psalm 69:8,
"I have become estranged from my brothers,
And an alien to my mother's sons."

David's life seems to be one of extreme loneliness, rejection and isolation.

When Samuel went to the house of Jesse to anoint a new king, Jesse had his seven sons (1 Samuel 16:10a) pass before the prophet. (David was not called or included in this event.) The seven sons were rejected by God (1 Samuel 16:10b). This caused Samuel to ask Jesse, "Are all the young men here?" Jesse replied, "There remains the youngest and he is keeping the sheep." It seems that Jesse kept David away from the family home and family life as much as possible, but despite Jesse's cold heart towards David, he did do one thing for David that was going to be the catalyst for the deliverance of Judah and the Nation of Israel (Genesis 17:12-13). Eight days after David's birth, his father would have had him circumcised! This made David a son of the covenant (like every other male in Israel). He was now in a generational blood covenant with YAHWEH, and the two foundational concepts of the covenant were "protection and prosperity"!

"Study the Blood!"

In 1 Samuel 17:1-58, we have the account of David and Goliath. In verse 26 David asks a blood covenant question, "Who is this uncircumcised Philistine, that he should defy the army of Israel?"

In David's mind he had already defeated Goliath, not because of the anointing, but because of the blood covenant. "Do not be afraid, I am your shield and your exceedingly great reward!" In 1 Samuel 17:34-37, David gives King Saul his testimony about killing the lion and bear with his bare hands (acknowledging the Lord's blood covenant protection).

So let us look at these events, because they are extremely relevant to us today.

"Blessed be God most High who has delivered your enemies into your hands!"

As a young shepherd boy (in David's time), not only were there lions and bears, but also leopards, wolves, foxes, poisonous snakes and scorpions. Danger and death was a serious daily possibility for young David, and for a father to send his young son out into that wild, hostile environment, day and night, without any weapons or protection, indicated very clearly that David's father and brothers wanted him dead!

Declaration!

The Lord is my shepherd
I shall not want!
It is God who arms me with strength!
He is my refuge and my fortress!
In Him I will put my trust!

David's encounters with lions and bears all happened before he was anointed by Samuel!

I was Born Again in August 1985, and from that moment until the writing of this section (2021), I have heard many excellent teachings on "The Anointing" (my two favourite teachers on the anointing are Kenneth Copeland and Benny Hinn).

I am a great believer in the anointing, because, as it says in Isaiah 10:27, "The yoke is destroyed because of the anointing." In Luke 4:18-19, Jesus declares himself as "the anointed one" (read also 1 John 2:27), but David didn't kill lions and bears because of the anointing.

The supernatural strength and ability to kill the lion and bears that were attempting to steal David's sheep came through "the blood covenant" that God made with Abram/Abraham!

God is eternally committed to all who are in a blood covenant with Him!

Every male in Israel who has been circumcised in the flesh was in a blood covenant with Almighty God. If you are Born Again, then you have been circumcised in the heart by the Holy Spirit (Romans 2:29) and you are also in an amazing "New Blood Covenant" with Jesus as the Guarantee (Hebrews 7:22). The Covenant that we are in is far, far greater than the covenant David was in. The lion, bear, leopard, wolves, foxes, snakes and scorpions that try to steal (John 10:10, Ephesians 6:12) from us have no protection against men and women who have "faith in the Blood"! So, in these encounters, David was "Untouchable"!

"Study the Blood!"
"The Keys are in the Blood!"

Now let us move on to David's encounter with Goliath!

David's question was, "Who is this uncircumcised Philistine?" (1Samuel 17:26c) This is not a question for information, this is a statement of derision (ridicule, scorn and contempt). David is declaring Goliath's total inability (uncircumcised) to stand against a man who has faith in a covenant keeping God!

David's second statement, "That he (Goliath) should defile the armies of the living (blood covenant) God?"

The amazing fact about David's last statement is that all Israelite soldiers (including Saul) were also in a blood covenant (by circumcision) with YAHWEH-SABAOTH, the Lord of Hosts. Any one of the Israelite soldiers (including Saul) could have faced Goliath and defeated him on the basis of the blood covenant God made with Abram, "I am your Shield!" The problem with Saul and the armies of Israel was "intimidation". This was nearly a repeat performance of the ten spies and the Israelites at the River Jordan, but in this case Yahweh has a man who has faith in the blood covenant!

Personal Testimony

This is a two realities testimony (while I was at a Watcher's Meeting in my city) on how the enemy uses the false evidence of intimidation to slow and stop the church.

The meeting had been going for about thirty

minutes. I was sitting in a comfortable chair near the back of the room. The next moment I am standing on the deck of a large sailing ship out in the ocean. There is an angel standing beside me, and out to my left also on the ocean, were many other sailing ships (of all sizes) and we were all heading in the same direction, towards a distant shoreline. As the wind filled the sails, we seemed to be travelling at great speed. As we got closer to the shoreline, I started to make out large black shapes. The only natural way I can describe them is that they resembled the standing stones on Easter Island, or the large standing stones of Stonehenge. Between each standing stone (the height of a four-story house) was a gap, large enough for an adult to pass through! I asked the angel, "What are they?" He answered, "They are standing stones of intimidation." Then he said, "At this point most of God's people either stop moving forward or turnaround and go back!" As I looked out at the other boats I could see what the angel had said was already starting to happen. Some of the boats had lowered their sails, let down their anchors and had come to a stop. Others had turned around and were heading back the way they had come. I looked at the angel and asked him, "What is the strategy to overcome this?" The angel looked at me as if I had asked a ridiculous question. He answered quite sternly, "Keep moving forward!" It was then that I received a deeper level of understanding. The large, black standing stones were there to intimidate the captain (leader) and crew of each ship (church), but the reality is, these standing stones had no power or authority to stop any of the ships from landing or to stop the crew from disembarking and moving forward.

So, the key strategy (the correct approach in achieving the desired, targeted purpose) in defeating intimidation is, "keep moving forward!"

The encounter ended there and I was back in the meeting room.

"Study the Blood!"

Let us now look at Psalm 23. This Psalm was written by one of God's "Untouchables" under the inspiration of the Holy Spirit. David, a warrior, king and prophet, recorded this Psalm. The two main principles of a blood covenant, protection and prosperity are clearly seen throughout this Psalm. Also, there are at least nine blood covenant names of God revealed in Psalm 23! Where God reveals one of His blood covenant names, he is revealing his:

1. Position
2. Authority

3. Character
4. Honour

Psalm 23 is a blood covenant song and it starts with:

- The Lord is my shepherd (protection) – Jehovah-Roi!
- I shall not want (prosperity) – Jehovah Jireh!
- He makes me to lie down (protection) in green pastures (prosperity) – Jehovah-Shalom!
- He leads me (protection) beside the still waters (prosperity) – Jehovah-Shalom!
- He restores my soul (protection and prosperity) – Jehovah-Rapha!
- He leads me (protection) in the paths of Righteousness (prosperity) – Jehovah-Tsidkenu!
- Yea, though I walk through the valley of the shadow of death, I will fear no evil (protection)!
- For You are with me – Jehovah-Shammah!
- Your rod and Your staff – Jehovah-Sabaoth!
- They comfort me (protection)!
- You prepare a table before me (prosperity) in the

presence of my enemies (protection) – Jehovah-Nissi!

- You anoint my head with oil (protection) – Jehovah M'kaddesh!
- My cup runs over (prosperity)!
- Surely goodness and mercy shall follow me all the days of my life (protection and prosperity)!
- And I will dwell in the house of the Lord forever (Protection and Prosperity)!

Let us quickly look at a very significant event in King David's life; it was the return of the Ark to Jerusalem. After a disastrous first attempt (2 Samuel 6:1-11), David returns to the House of Obed-Edom a second time to collect the Ark, but this time he did it God's way. The Levites carried the Ark and David sacrificed oxen and sheep every six paces (2 Samuel 6:13) back to Jerusalem. This was a distance of about twelve miles and the total quantity of blood shed over the distance would have been at least three thousand gallons!

David sacrificed every six paces, six is the number of man, and the great quantity of blood that was shed by David every six paces is symbolic of the Blood of Jesus that was shed for every man and woman who is a blood relation of Adam. The Blood that Jesus shed on Earth and poured out in Heaven was not for archangels, angels, elders or living creatures, it was for one type of creation only, and that was man! We, like all those who followed David (through the blood) back to Jerusalem with the Ark, must on a daily basis walk in the Power of the Blood of the Lamb! The Blood is for us and we are called by the eternal spirit to live, move and have our being (by faith) in the ever living, all powerful, eternal Blood of Jesus!

In Hebrews 13:8, it says, "Jesus Christ is the same yesterday, today and forever." The Blood Covenant God of Abram/Abraham, Isaac, Jacob, Moses and David has never changed. All He requires is a man or woman who will stand on His Blood Covenant Word, and He will move Heaven or Hell on their behalf.

1 Kings 2:10, tells us that, "David rested with his fathers." Throughout David's life, no wild beast or enemy armies could harm him, because of his faith in his Blood Covenant God. David was "Untouchable"!

Declaration!

For by you I can run through a troop,
I can leap over a wall!

It is you who arms me with strength!

It is you who makes my way perfect!

It is you who sets me on high!

7

Jesus and the Walk of Blood!

The biblical history of man starts in Genesis 2:7, "And the Lord God (Yahweh Elohim) formed man of the dust of the ground, and breathed into his nostrils the breath of life; and man became a living being."

In Genesis 2:8, it says, "The Lord God (Yahweh Elohim) planted a garden eastward in Eden, and there He put the man whom He had formed."

Adam surrendered his will and handed dominion of planet earth and all life and resources of planet earth over to Satan in a garden! Since that moment, man lost his ability to overcome evil (internal and external) by the power of his own will. This is why we need to get Born Again. The restoration of man's will can only come through and by the Blood of Jesus!

Jesus came as the last Adam (1 Corinthians 15:45b) to restore in a garden what Adam lost in a garden, "dominion"; the ability to say "No" to anything that is offered to us from the "Tree of the Knowledge of Good and Evil", to say "Yes" to that which comes from the "Tree of Life".

"The Life is in the Blood!"

In Matthew, Mark and Luke you will find a brief account of what happened in the Garden of Gethsemane, but, for me, there seemed to be a lot more to this event than was actually said. So, I started to pray in tongues for more insight into what actually happened. The first instruction I received from the Holy Spirit (and He should know because He was there) was to call this account (as far as this book is concerned), "The Battle of Gethsemane". My next question was, "Why?" The answer came very quickly, "Because Jesus was about to fight the greatest and most ferocious battle of His earthly life up to this time in the garden, even to the point of death, but He overcame, not as God, but as a man!"

So let us look at the phenomenal battle which Jesus fought (on our behalf) in Gethsemane!

"We do not wrestle against flesh and blood, but against principalities, powers, rulers of the darkness, and spiritual wickedness in the Heavenlies!"

The "Battle of Gethsemane" starts with Jesus and His disciples entering the Garden (about midnight) after celebrating the Passover and initiating what we call "The Lord's Supper" or "Communion". He tells most of His disciples to wait at a certain place in the Garden and then He continues walking on, taking Peter, James and John with Him (these are His three mighty men). The account in Matthew 26:37 says, "He began to be sorrowful, heavy and deeply disturbed". The Battle had begun!

Jesus was now coming under attack (in the soul realm) and was having to engage and resist (by faith) an invisible enemy. Remember Gethsemane means "Olive Press", a place of crushing!

In Luke's account, we are told that an Angel from heaven was sent (by the Father) to strengthen Jesus (Luke 22:43), then in the next verse (Luke 22:44) it says that Jesus was in "agony". (Remember Jesus is lying down on His face fighting the greatest battle of His earthly life.) The sorrow, heaviness, deep distress, agony (even to the point of death) that Jesus was experiencing wasn't natural, it was satanic, demonic and supernatural! The soul of Jesus, the mind of Jesus, the will of Jesus and the emotions of Jesus were under unrelenting, continuous, savage attack by demonic princes, powers and the dark forces of Hell, and they had only one purpose and that was to totally, completely and permanently break and shatter the will of Jesus, and to mentally and emotionally crush him (oil press) even to the point of death, even suicide!

Remember, Satan's only purpose in the lives of every man, woman and child on planet earth (seven billion) is to "Steal, kill and destroy!"

The battle in the soul, mind and emotions of Jesus was so intense and consuming that, in Luke's account, it says He (Jesus) sweated blood. Today, the medical term of this condition is "Hematohidrosis". This is caused when capillary blood vessels that feed the sweat glands rupture, causing them to exude blood. It occurs under conditions of extreme physical and emotional stress.

Remember, Jesus' Blood came from the Father, not from the earth, so the earth could not receive it back!

Remember, everything that Jesus went through in the "Battle of Gethsemane" He went through for us!

Personal Testimony One

The day when I gave my life to Christ was a Saturday (10th August 1985). After receiving Jesus as my Lord and Saviour, I felt tremendous, as if a huge weight had been lifted from me. Everything sparkled and looked cleansed and clean!

The man who explained repentance and the Cross to me (Robert Ward) gave me a Bible (NIV) and he wrote two verses in it, Romans 10:14-15 and 1 John 3:8b. I had never felt as happy and as emotionally free as I did on that amazing day!

After going to bed later that Saturday night (with the Bible next to the bed), I came under a vicious (about one o'clock in the morning), demonic attack. I didn't know it then, but I was about to experience my own "Battle of Gethsemane!" Being just Born Again, I had no idea how to defend myself against these demonic forces (also I knew nothing about being in a Blood Covenant). Satan and his government (Ephesians 6:12) uses our ignorance as a weapon against us. The oppression and the fear that gripped me was so intense, I felt as if I was about to die. Linda had to literally take me to Robert Ward's house for help (I took the Bible with me). It was about two o'clock in the morning.

After arriving at his house, Linda knocked and he opened the door and let us in (me, Linda and our two little boys, Allan, two and a half years, and Marc, six months). I explained the horrendous things that were happening (no details needed) and asked for help. After talking, Linda went home with the boys and Robert went back to bed, leaving me sitting in a chair in his living room at 3 o'clock in the morning.

The chair I was sitting in was facing a large dividing wall and, no sooner had everyone left, the wall disappeared (my eyes were open) and flying towards me out of a huge black expanse where the wall had been, was wave upon wave of demons (the closest description I can give is that they looked like harpies from Greek Mythology). I felt as if I was paralysed and was about to be taken into this blackness by those demons, then I heard a voice, "Paul, open the Bible", which I did and it opened up at Matthew 28:18. Then the voice said (the Holy Spirit), "Read it out aloud, until day break!" So I read out aloud, "And Jesus came and spoke to them saying, 'All authority has been given to Me in heaven and on earth.'" As I read the verse, the first wave of demonic spirits screamed, writhing and disappeared, and as I continually kept reading it out aloud, wave after wave of demonic spirits were overcome.

This went on until daybreak (about 5:30/5:45), that is when it all stopped. The demonic portal closed and the wall reappeared. I then quietly left the house and returned home.

I had learned some very valuable lessons, one being the kingdom of Hell has no defence against the now (Rhema) Word of God!

Now let us briefly turn our attention to the apostles; Peter, James and John, Jesus' three mighty men. What condition were they in when this epic supernatural battle was raging? They were asleep! At the time when Jesus needed the support of his three closest warriors, they had been totally immobilised. They were asleep, but this wasn't natural sleep. The atmosphere in the garden was thick with satanic and demonic oppression.

Personal Testimony Two

Very soon after getting Born Again (10th August 1985) I had a strong desire to read the Bible from Genesis to Revelation, but every time I picked up the Bible and started to read it (Genesis 1:1) I would fall asleep. No matter what time of the day it was, as soon as I started reading, my eyes would become heavy and I would fall asleep. This really concerned me because I knew I was meant to read the Bible from Genesis to Revelation, so I did some serious praying in tongues about it and this was the strategy I was given. "The next time you pick up the Bible to read, stand up, walk up and down your living room and read out aloud." So that is what I did (Isaiah 1:19; James 3:7) and it worked, a simple but very effective Heavenly strategy!

"We overcome by the Blood of the Lamb and the Word of our Testimony!"

I would now like to draw your attention to the fact that everything Jesus experienced, from the betrayal by Judas (in the Garden), his journey to Golgotha and his Crucifixion, all these events involved people (Jews and Romans), but in his epic battle in the Garden there were no people involved. In Luke 22:42 Jesus cries out, "Father, if it is Your will, take this cup away from Me; nevertheless not My will, but Your will, be done." This cry was never repeated by Jesus after the Battle of Gethsemane, despite the horrendous suffering, abuse, pain and rejection He was going to go through! The Blood that He shed in the battle of Gethsemane was for us, for the deliverance of our soul, mind and emotions from all and every satanic and demonic attack. From slight anxiety to massive mental and emotional breakdown, from small insecurities to extreme paranoia, from anxiety, PTSD and suicide.

Personal Testimony Three

31st October 1985 was my first experience of Halloween as a new believer (two months old). Without going into details, Halloween was a significant time in the generational lives of certain members of my family and myself (before I was Born Again).

Linda was out that night at a Bible study and the two boys were in bed asleep. It was then that I started to feel a build up of oppression, heaviness and an unpleasant awareness of heat, so I started to pray in tongues, but it became more and more intense. Once again "the battle" was on! After about an hour of the demonic oppression, I was physically and mentally exhausted and could hardly speak in tongues.

I was lying on the floor in the kitchen and a loud cruel voice was shouting at me repeatedly, "You still belong to me!" Then from somewhere within me I became aware of a statement rising up into my mind and the statement was, "No weapon formed against you can succeed, you shall prevail and every tongue that rises against you, you shall cast down!"

After my experience in August in Robert Ward's house, I knew exactly what to do. I needed to speak out what I had just received, so that is what I did. I focussed my mind on the now Word and started to speak it out, and this is what I said (repeatedly):

In the Name of Jesus, I declare that
No weapon formed against me can succeed.
I shall prevail!
Every tongue that rises up against me,
I cast down!

Finally, the voice was silenced, and after thirty minutes, all the oppression and heaviness had gone. Once again I had experienced that Hell has no defence against the now (Rhema) Word of God!

So, Jesus in the "battle" of Gethsemane won, overcame and stood victorious on our behalf, so that no weapon formed against your soul, mind and emotions can succeed, so that we will always prevail and cast down every tongue that has risen against us (past, present and future)!

Declarations!

In the Name of Jesus
and because of the Blood of the Lamb,
my soul is restored!

In the Name of Jesus
and because of the Blood of the Lamb,
my mind is renewed!

In the Name of Jesus
and because of the Blood of the Lamb,
my will is redeemed!

In the Name of Jesus
and because of the Blood of the Lamb,
as He is, so are we in this world!

In this next section of Jesus' Walk of Blood, we will look at the scourging of Jesus and its profound importance for us today! The only account of Jesus being scourged by the Romans is in John 19:1, Matthew, Mark and Luke don't mention it at all, but its importance cannot be ignored or underestimated.

The Roman scourge was an instrument of punishment not execution, but during the brutal and cruel process, prisoners often died. (Remember, Jesus had just come from being interrogated by the high priest and from the Garden of Gethsemane.) The scourging could last as long as the Roman soldiers wanted it to, there was no limitation on how many stripes they could lay upon a man's back! The injury that Jesus experienced during the scourging was horrendous, the flesh was ripped from his back, severe bruising of the lungs (possible puncture and lung collapse), bleeding in the chest cavity, lacerated liver, massive blood loss, accute dehydration and traumatic shock. This event would have killed any other man very early on.

Jesus was an innocent man being punished, and the terrible punishment he was receiving (scourging) was on our behalf! In Isaiah 53:5 it says, "He (Messiah) was wounded for our transgressions (rebellion)." The definition of the word "wounded" is suffering injury or bodily harm through laceration!

"The punishment for our peace (shalom) was upon Him." Shalom is a very deep and powerful word, but basically it means deliverance, health, prosperity and favour! Then in Isaiah it says, "By His stripes we are healed" and in 1 Peter 2:24 it says, "By whose stripes you were healed." Both words "healed" mean cured, repaired and thoroughly made whole!

Jesus went through this vicious, brutal and traumatic experience for us, so that we, by putting our faith in Him and His Blood, could be delivered from our transgressions (rebellion) and could live a life here on earth of victory, health, prosperity and great favour.

Upon His back He took my stripes,
my pain and agony.
Upon His back He took my stripes
and suffered to set me free.
By His wounds I am healed.
By His wounds I am whole.
No greater love has been seen,
Than the Lamb who suffered for my soul!

I will finish this section of "The Walk of Blood" with a statement, "Any so called man, woman or denomination that preaches or teaches that there is no healing or deliverance in, by or through the Blood of Jesus, the Lamb of God, is a mouthpiece for an anti-Christ spirit! Both the Prophet Isaiah and the Apostle Peter (the first Pope if you are a Catholic), by the inspiration of the Holy Spirit, agree that,

"By His wounds we are healed!"

Testimony One

The person's name will not be given only her initials.

LB "I had a very large boil on my leg. The Holy Spirit said, 'Plead the Blood and then go and have a bath.' After my bath, the boil had completely disappeared!"

Testimony Two

From NH "In October 2020 I heard from my son who was house sharing in London that his three housemates had Covid-19 and that all of them (including my son) had to go into quarantine for ten days. As a mother and woman of faith, I immediately started to plead the Blood over him every day, and by faith I covered the lintels, the door posts and his room with the Blood of the Lamb. Then after ten days I received a very happy phone call from him saying, 'The quarantine is over and somehow I didn't get it, no symptoms at all!'"

"The Blood of the Lamb is just as powerful today in the 21st Century as it was in the 1st Century!"

Testimony Three

This is from LA who is seventeen years old and in my own words:

"I was on my way home from the City Centre by metro with my mates. As the metro entered the tunnel I could smell smoke. Suddenly the metro stopped and tilted, making a loud noise. All the lights went out, the engine stopped and the metro carriage started to fill with smoke. Everyone was screaming, some were crying, there were people calling their families by mobile in sheer panic. The mechanism under the carriage was on fire and sparks were shooting along the window. I started praying in tongues and the lights came back on! Then God told me to get down on one knee, lay my hands on the floor and pray in tongues. I did exactly what he said and blocked out all the screams and crying. The engine restarted and the smoke stopped, the sparks ended and the screaming stopped. God then told me to trust Him and that we would all get off safely. I covered the passengers in the Blood and sprinkled it over the metro carriage. Eventually the staff evacuated everyone and guided us through the tunnels. I was the last to get off and thanked the staff, but more importantly I thanked Jesus that His Blood had protected us!

Section three about "Jesus and His Walk of Blood" is about the Crown of Thorns. Firstly we will take a brief look at the physical side of the brutal encounter. Jesus had just gone through the "Battle of Gethsemane", sweated blood, He had been interrogated by the high priest, chief priests, elders and scribes (Matthew 26:57). Then, early in the morning, He was taken into the praetorium where he was interrogated by Pontius Pilate. Next He was handed on to the Roman soldiers who brutally scourged Him, then they twisted a Crown of Thorns and put it on his head (John 19:2). The Crown of Thorns would have been forcefully put upon Jesus' head so that the thorns would have pierced the flesh and embedded themselves in the skull of Jesus, then they spat on Him and struck Him on the head! Remember, Jesus is standing before them with His back ripped open, massive bleeding, acute dehydration and in traumatic shock (all for us). Striking Jesus on the head would have caused him excruciating pain across His face and deep into his ears. Every time He moved His head there would have been intense pain. The thorns would have cut into the blood vessels in the head area, they would have caused heavy bleeding, vomiting and an increase in the traumatic shock He was already suffering! This "Crown of Thorns" would be embedded in the head of Jesus all the way to and upon the Cross!

"Study the Blood!"

Every drop of Blood Jesus shed from the Garden to the Cross has eternal value for every believer, on earth and in Heaven. Thorns are first mentioned in the Bible in Genesis 3:18, and they are a sign and a symbol of the curse. Anything that is produced by the hand of man is in a fallen state and is unacceptable in the eyes of God (Genesis 2:2-5). Blood is the only acceptable offering that can be given! Thorns symbolise pain, toil, labour, self-effort, works, lack, shortage, poverty and rejection. Matthew, Mark and John (a bench of three) all give an account of "Jesus' Coronation" (a ceremony to crown a sovereign) at the hand of the gentiles (Romans). The Romans bowed their knee before Him and said, "Hail, King of the Jews" and He was the King of the Jews, but when they placed the "Crown of Thorns" upon His head, things changed because of the "Crown of Thorns". Jesus became "King of the curse", "King of the cursed", and "King of the fallen earth", Jesus became "Lord of the fallen", "The King of thorns"! The curse and everything connected to it was placed on the head of Jesus! He was the only one who had the authority to wear it. He was the only one who was authorised to carry the responsibility of a cursed earth, and a cursed humanity!

Jesus' Crown of Thorns won back our prosperity! The symbol of poverty (thorns) was placed upon the head of the second Adam (Jesus). When those thorns pierced His head, the blood that flowed was for our redemption from poverty. We were cursed with poverty, lack and shortage by the sweat of Adam's brow, but we have been redeemed from the curse of poverty by the Blood on Jesus' brow! 2 Corinthians 8:9, "For you know the grace of our Lord Jesus Christ, that though He was rich (ploo-tos), yet for your sakes He became poor (pto-khos), that you through His poverty (pto-khos) might become rich (ploo-tos)."

If you confess with your mouth what you believe in your heart about the Blood that was shed by the Lamb of God, then the Holy Spirit will legally move on your behalf, because the Spirit and the Blood are in agreement!

Declarations!

I declare in the Name of Jesus
and because of the Blood of the Lamb,
I am anointed to prosper!

I declare in the Name of Jesus
and because of the Blood of the Lamb,
I am financially flourishing in every area of life!

I declare in the Name of Jesus
and because of the Blood of the Lamb,
all generational poverty
has been removed from my life
and I now live, move and have my being
in Kingdom prosperity and success!

Joshua 1:8,
"Do not let my Word depart from your mouth,

meditate on it day and night,
observe to do all that is written in it.
Then you will make your way prosperous
and you will have good success."

Psalm 1:2-3,
"His delight is in the word of the Lord,
And in His word he meditates day and night.
He is like a tree planted by the rivers of water,
That brings forth fruit in its season,
Whose leaf does not wither;
And whatever he does shall prosper."

8

The Blood of His Cross

We are now at the final four stages of Jesus' Walk of Blood: The Crucifixion!

Firstly, let us go back to the Prophet John's declaration in John 1:29, "Behold! The Lamb of God who takes away the sin of the world!" This statement is powerful and deep, so let us first look at "The Lamb of God". Any lamb that was to be offered up as a sacrifice to God had to be the best of the flock (Genesis 4:4; Leviticus 3:6; Numbers 6:14). Jesus was the perfect, spotless, sinless Lamb of God! This statement that the Prophet John made would have had a profound effect on his disciples who were there with him. Being Jews, they knew by their own national history and personal experience, that a lamb that was going to be offered to God as a sacrifice, firstly had to have its throat cut, then the blood would be drained and sprinkled upon the altar, and it would only be acceptable to God if the altar was holy. The blood of the sacrificial lamb that was sprinkled upon the altar made the altar holy (Exodus 29:37c). The altar had to be sanctified by blood if it was to possess the power to sanctify whatever touches it!

"The Cross was the Altar!"
"Study the Blood!"
"The Life is in the Blood!"

John's next statement was, "who takes away the sin of the world!"

Jesus, being the legitimate King of Israel and the Lamb of God, was going to be sacrificed on behalf of the whole Jewish nation and also on behalf of the whole gentile world. In order for this to happen, the highest authority in Israel had to inspect the sacrificial lamb, and the highest authority in the gentile world also had to inspect the sacrificial lamb (the lamb had to be faultless). So, in Mark 14:55 it says, "The chief priests and all the council sought testimony against Jesus to put Him to death, **BUT FOUND NONE!**" Jesus was innocent! Jesus was faultless! Next He had to be inspected by the highest authority in the gentile world. This was the Emperor Tiberius (because Rome was the global super power of the day), but the emperor was in Rome, so in Luke 23:1 it says that, "The multitude arose and took Him (Jesus) to Pilate." Pilate was the legal, delegated representative of Emperor Tiberius. When Pontius Pilate made a governmental decision, it was as if the Emperor had personally spoken himself! After speaking to Jesus, he made the statement (on behalf of the whole gentile world), "So Pilate said to the chief priests and the crowd, "**I FIND NO FAULT IN THIS MAN**!"" (Luke 23:4) The Jewish nation and the gentile world was in perfect agreement, "The Lamb was innocent! The Lamb was faultless! The Lamb was acceptable! The Lamb was ready to be sacrificed!"

The great difference between all the blood sacrifices that had been offered to God before Jesus (The Lamb of God) was that their blood had been drained and they were already dead before they were placed on the altar. Jesus, the Lamb of God, was to be put upon the Altar (the Cross) alive. He was going to be "A Living Sacrifice" for the Jews and the gentiles. This great honour of placing the Lamb of God on the altar was given to the Romans representing the gentile world.

In order for Jesus (The Lamb of God) to be an

acceptable sacrifice, the Altar (the Cross) had to be sprinkled with His Blood before He died. This was done in two stages. It says in John 19:17 that Jesus carried his own cross to Golgotha (The Place of the Skull). The Latin word is "Patibulum", and it means "crossbeam", so the "crossbeam" was placed upon the shoulders of Jesus. Remember His back had been ripped open and mutilated by the scourge and upon His head was still the Crown of Thorns, so His Blood, the Blood of the Sacrificial Lamb, was now on one part of the Cross. At Golgotha His Blood would cover the whole Altar (The Cross).

As a form of capital punishment, Crucifixion was widespread. Teams of well trained Roman soldiers carried out the Crucifixion. Each team consisted of the "exactor mortis" or centurion and four soldiers called the "quarterino". Crucifixions were carried out in full view of the public. The nails used were made of iron and were about nine inches long. It is impossible to imagine the tremendous pain, agony and trauma that Jesus was going through (on our behalf) due to massive blood loss and acute dehydration.

To be crucified, Jesus would have been thrown to the ground and made to lie on His heavily scourged back. Then He would have been held down as the

Roman soldiers started to hammer the iron nails into His hands; the right hand (stage four) and the left hand (stage five). The pain and the agony would have been beyond anything we could imagine, "He was pierced for our transgressions!" (Rebellion!) Then the Roman soldiers would have lifted Him up by the legs inserting the crossbeam (PATIBULUM) into the mortice on top of the upright. The Roman soldiers would then have bent His knees until the feet of Jesus were flush to the upright. Then they would hammer in the iron nails through the feet of Jesus pinning them to the post (stage six). Now the Blood of the Lamb is upon the Altar (The Cross) and the sacrifice is acceptable!

Remember, Jesus' Blood did not come out of the earth, so the earth could not receive it back. Jesus' Blood came from His Father and the nature of Blood is to always return to its place of origin!

"Study the Blood!"

In the Garden of Eden, God (Elohim) placed all global authority into the hands of Adam. In Psalm 8:6 it says, "You have made him to have dominion over the works of Your hands!" When Adam rebelled, he handed it all over to Satan and Satan became god of the world. As the Roman soldiers hammered in the iron nails through the right and left hand of Jesus, the Blood of the Lamb of God flowed and His Blood restored our dominion and authority! It is "**FAITH IN THE BLOOD**" that causes us to overcome (Romans 12:11). The hands of Jesus were nailed down so our hands could be free. The Constitution of our Kingdom states that "We have been redeemed by the Blood of Jesus" (Ephesians 1:7). Our authority has been redeemed! Our dominion has been redeemed! Our hands have been redeemed! It is time to take our hands (2 Corinthians 6:2) and lay them on the sick, the demonised and the dead, and claim God's Blood Covenant promise with authority in the Name (position, authority and character) of Jesus!!

Job 22:30, "He will deliver one who is not innocent. Yes, He will be delivered by the purity of Your hands!" All our purity comes through and by "The Blood of the Lamb", not by any works of ours!

Jesus feet were immobilised (by the iron nails) so that our feet can be released. The Blood of Jesus that flowed from His feet release us to "Go" (Matthew 28:19; Mark 16:15; Romans 10:15; 2 Corinthians 6:2). The Blood that flowed from the feet of Jesus restores our authority and territorial dominion (Joshua 1:3; Mark 5:10; Luke 10:19).

"Study the Blood!"

Before we look at the piercing of Jesus' side, it would benefit us to look briefly at Isaiah 52:14 and Isaiah 53. These scriptures are describing prophetically the Crucifixion of Jesus and what He achieved for us. Isaiah 52:14 says about Jesus on the Cross, "His visage (appearance) was marred (disfigured) more than any man!" By the time Jesus was nailed to the Cross His physical body had gone through so much punishment, torture, abuse and brutality, that He no longer looked like a man. The level of disfigurement He was suffering had never been seen before nor would ever be seen again, and all that was done for us!

Question: Does this mean that Jesus took all forms of human disfigurement, no matter what the cause, upon Himself?

Answer: YES!

"By His wounds we are healed!"

Disfigurement through violence, disease, accident, death or in the womb, was taken for us on the Cross by Jesus. It was an act of unparalleled love shown towards His greatest creation, man.

Love is the answer, love is the key
Love is the power that will set My creation free!

Love is the answer, love is the key
Love is the Way of Liberty!

Don't look back, don't stand still
Walk in love and fulfil My Will!

"By His wounds we are healed!"

A good Biblical example of the restoration of someone who was severely disfigured and also died was the Apostle Paul in Lystra (Acts 14:20). Paul was stoned and the injuries through being stoned are brutal; broken bones, cracked skull, broken jaw, teeth and nose, bruising (internal bleeding), lacerated skin and eventually death. Also, in Paul's case, they dragged his dead body out of the City (this would have caused more of Paul's skin to be shredded), but because of what Jesus did from the Garden to the Cross, the disciples gathered around Paul's dead, disfigured and broken body and, by faith in the "Blood of the Lamb", they prayed (I believe in Tongues) and his spirit returned, he rose up alive, healed and totally restored! Paul was the only Apostle to be martyred twice; once in Lystra and then in Rome!

"By His wounds we are healed!"

In Isaiah 53:1, the question is asked, "Who has believed our report?" In our day it could read, "Who has believed in the Blood?" It is those who have "Faith in the Blood" that "The arm (power) of the Lord is revealed! Faith is the key that opens the door for experiential revelation of the Power of God."

"All things are possible for those who believe!"

PRAYER

I pray that the God of our Lord Jesus Christ,
The Father of Glory,
Will give you the Spirit of Wisdom
and Revelation
in the Experiential knowledge of Him,
and that the eyes of your understanding
will be enlightened that you may know,
by revelation and experience,
the full reality of Isaiah 53
and the full Power of the Blood of the Lamb!

"Study the Blood!"

"The Life is in the Blood!"

By meditating on Isaiah 53, you will see how all

encompassing the Blood of the Lamb and the sacrifice was. Nothing was missed or overlooked. Everything the Father sent Jesus to do on Earth as the Sacrificial Lamb was finalised on the Altar (Cross). When Jesus said in John 19:30, "It is finished", His earthly ministry in Israel was complete! In Isaiah 53:12b, it says He (Jesus) will divide the spoil (plunder) with the strong (AW-TSOOM – powerful, mighty).

Question: Who are the strong?

The answer is in Daniel 11:32b, "Those who know (by revelation and experience) their God shall be strong (KHAW-ZAK – mighty, valiant, courageous)." In order to know God by revelation and experience you have to have access to God, and that only comes through and by the "Blood of the Lamb" (Hebrews 10:19), and that first encounter with the Blood comes with the New Birth! Faith in Christ enables the Holy Spirit to apply the Blood and totally, completely and eternally wash your sins away (past, present and future). Psalm 103:12 says, "As far as the east is from the west, so far has He removed our transgressions (sin) from us!"

Isaiah 43:25, "I am He who blots out your transgressions for My own sake (covenant); and I will not remember your sins."

Hebrews 8:12b, "Their sins and their lawless deeds I will remember no more!"

When we get Born Again, we are NOT sinners saved by grace, we were sinners and we were saved by grace, but now we are (by the Blood):

1. Sons and Daughters of God!

2. Kings and Royal Priests in the Order of Melchizedek!

3. Saints!

4. Citizens of Heaven!

5. Salt!

6. Light!

7. Ambassadors of Reconciliation!

8. Shields of the Earth!

"The Life is in the Blood!"
"Study the Blood!"

The account in John 19:34, "The piercing of Jesus' side" is the seventh and final stage of the vicious shedding of Jesus' Blood. It is important to remember that throughout Israel's history, not one bone of any of the sacrifices to God was broken (Exodus 12:46), "Nor shall you break one of its bones." The Passover lamb was not to have its legs broken!

Numbers 9:12, "Nor break one of its bones!"

Psalm 34:20, "He guards all his bones; not one of them is broken!"

Despite the horrendous brutality that Jesus went through from the Garden to the Cross, not one of His bones were broken. The Body of Jesus wasn't broken for us, it was given for us!

"Study the Blood!"

In John 19:33, the Roman soldiers were going to break Jesus' legs, but they found Him already dead. All His bones were protected (Psalm 34:20). The first promise in a Blood Covenant is "protection". Faith in His Blood will enable the Holy Spirit to legally protect all your bones and the bones of your household! Strong, healthy bones are a Blood Covenant right for every son and daughter of God!

The Hymn writer in 1772 wrote:

"There is a fountain filled with Blood,
Drawn from Immanuel's veins,

And sinners plunged beneath that flood,
Lose all their guilty stains!"

I will now give you two testimonies. The names of the people involved will not be given, only their initials.

Testimony One

NH "I hadn't been saved long when I had a vision (August 1997), actually it was more real than a vision as it felt like I was there. I remembered it was dawn, I was standing at the foot of the Cross, ankle deep in a River of Blood that was flowing downhill. I looked up and saw where the Blood was coming from. It was Jesus and He looked down at me from the Cross and said, "I did this for you (N)!" He called me by my name. I was totally blown away! There were lots of tears and a lot of healing going on. So, every time I drink the wine in communion, I see Jesus looking down at me from the Cross saying, "I DID THIS FOR YOU!""

Testimony Two

SS "The Blood still flows!"

"At Church I had the following vision, which was very clear and vivid. I saw a hill and the Cross, and from the Cross a River of Blood was flowing and I heard the words, "The Blood is still flowing!""

The River of the Blood of Jesus is still flowing. You may be standing on the river bank or, like NH, you may be ankle deep in the River of the Blood of Jesus, but no matter where you are, the Holy Spirit is calling your name and He wants to take you deeper into the River of the Blood of Jesus!

"We overcome by the Blood of the Lamb and the Word of our Testimony!"

Finally, I would like to declare that Jesus was the greatest of all the "Untouchables" ever to walk the Earth! The question might arise in the minds of the readers, "How?", considering all the violent and brutal treatment Jesus experienced, which finally culminated in His Crucifixion. The key to that answer is in John 10:17-18, Jesus says, "Therefore My Father loves me, because I lay down my life that I may take it again. No one takes it from Me, but I lay it down of Myself. I have the power to lay it down and I have the power to take it again. This command I have received from My Father."

There are a number of accounts in the Gospels where Satan had attempted to kill Jesus. In Luke 4:28-30, it's the account of all the members of Jesus' home synagogue being filled with murderous rage, taking Jesus to the edge of a cliff to throw Him down and kill Him. In Luke 4:30 it says, "Jesus passed through the midst of them." He didn't walk around the murderous crowd, He walked through them, and there was nothing they could do about it. Jesus was "Untouchable"!

In Luke 8:22-25 is the account of Jesus in the boat with His disciples. He is asleep when a great storm arose. This is not a natural storm. The elemental spirits of air and water joined forces to kill Jesus! In Luke 8:24 the disciples wake Jesus up and it says, "He rebuked the wind and the raging water and there was calm." This satanic attack failed and Jesus the "Untouchable" carried on His mission to Gadarenes!

The third example of Jesus being "Untouchable" is John 10:31-39. The Jews were picking up stones to kill Jesus, but in verse 39 it says, "Therefore they sought to seize Him, but He escaped out of their hands." The angry Jewish mob who wanted to stone Jesus to death couldn't even lay a finger on Him. He was "Untouchable"!

Genesis 15:1, "I am your shield!" So, everything Jesus went through from the Garden to the Cross He allowed, so that the scriptures could be fulfilled, but at any time (Matthew 26:53) He could have said,

"Enough is enough", but thank God, He didn't, He finished His course, so that we, his Blood bought sons and daughters, can walk forward as one of His "Untouchables"!

9

The Return of the Blood

Let us start Chapter nine with this statement that, "It is the nature of blood to return to its original source or place of origin!"

"Study the Blood!"

Not one drop of Blood that Jesus shed from the Garden to the cross came from Adam or out of the earth (Genesis 2:7). Jesus' Blood came from His Father who was in Heaven!

When Adam rebelled against God (Elohim), Satan became his father and his blood was poisoned by sin which resulted in death (Romans 5:12). Six thousand years later, mankind is still dying because of poisoned (sin) blood. However, the Blood of Jesus, every cell in the Blood of Jesus and the DNA of Jesus was, and still is, without sin and totally pure. This is why in John 14:30 Jesus said, "The ruler (Satan) of this world (kos-mos) has nothing in me." So, because the Blood of Jesus did not come from Adam and out of the earth, the earth could not receive it back. Satan had no legal claim on Jesus. The Blood of Jesus came from the Father, out of Heaven by the Holy Spirit, and it was to be returned to its place of origin, and the only person who could do that was God, the Holy Spirit! He gathered up all the shed Blood of Jesus (from the Garden to the Cross) and kept it until the resurrection of Jesus on the third day! In 2 Peter 3:8 it says, "DO NOT FORGET THIS ONE THING, THAT WITH THE LORD, ONE DAY IS AS A THOUSAND YEARS AND A THOUSAND YEARS AS ONE DAY!"

As I write this Chapter, it is the month of February 2021, two thousand and twenty-one years since Jesus was raised from the dead by the Holy Spirit. It is the beginning of the third millennium and we are all in the very early stages of the "third day"!

Question: What was the first thing to happen on the third day?

The first thing that happened on the third day was that the Spirit of Jesus was returned to the physical body of Jesus by the Holy Spirit. Jesus was now back in His body (you are a spirit in a body). Next He stood up and stepped out of His grave clothes (they were no longer needed), but He was still in the tomb. In Matthew 28:2 it says, "There was a great earthquake and an angel of the Lord descended from Heaven and rolled back the stone from the door and sat on it!" (The resurrected Jesus could have easily moved the stone himself, but even after His resurrection, He was still totally dependant on His Father.) Now He can step out of the tomb. All these events are signs for us who are living in the early part of the third day!

1. The return of the Spirit to the real body of Christ!

2. The Body of Christ stepping out of all the grave clothes that they have been wrapped in and trapped in!

3. A significant increase in angelic activity in the removing of all barriers to the progress and freedom of the Body of Christ!

Jesus is now ready for the next part of His mission and that is to pour out His Blood on the Mercy Seat in the Heavenly Tabernacle. It says in Hebrews 4:14

that Jesus, our Great High Priest, passed through the Heavens. Remember (Matthew 28:18) all power and authority belongs to Jesus (Colossians 2:10). Satan and his (Ephesians 6:12) kingdom has been defeated, disarmed, stripped and humiliated!

2 Timothy 1:10b tells us that, "Death has been abolished" (kat-arg-eh-o to be rendered totally useless, to be made of non-effect and to be made totally void), and in 1 John 3:8b it says, "The reason the Son of God (Jesus) was made manifest was to destroy all the works of the devil!"

Jesus, as He stood outside of the tomb, is now (Revelation 1:8, 18) the Alpha and Omega, the Almighty and has the keys to death and Hades!!!

"Study the Blood!"

I now would like to draw your attention to the fact at the resurrection (the third day) there was no Blood in Jesus' body. All of His Blood had to be poured out on the Mercy Seat in the Holy of Holies! Jesus said to His disciples in Luke 24:39, "Behold My hands and My feet. Handle Me and see, for a Spirit does not have flesh and bones as you see I have!" The Life is in the Blood and the resurrection life that is eternally in the Blood of Jesus is for all mankind (if they choose by faith to accept the Lamb of God into their lives).

Jesus' physical body of flesh and bone is empty of Blood, but full of the Glory of God. In 2 Corinthians 13:4b it says that, "He (Jesus) lives by the Power of God!"

"The Life is in the Blood!"
"The Keys are in the Blood!"

From the fall (rebellion) of Adam until the Crucifixion and Resurrection of Jesus, the Heavens were governed by Satan and his kingdom (Ephesians 6:12). Through one man's (Adam) rebellion, Satan and his kingdom gained legal access and authority to multiple, invisible realms, dimensions and spheres that were and are continually interacting with planet earth and all life upon it (Mark 8:24; Isaiah 47; Daniel 10:12-20). One man, Adam, handed it all to Satan, and one man (Jesus) took it all back!

Jesus passed through all the heavens (Hebrew 4:14), realms, dimensions and spheres.

The all powerful, almighty, victorious, overcoming King, cleansing everything with His Blood! As Blood bought, Blood washed sons and daughters of God, everything that Adam handed over to Satan has been redeemed, restored and returned to us through and by the Blood of Jesus.

After passing through the heavens, Jesus (carrying His own Blood) entered the Heavenly Tabernacle on our behalf!

On Earth, the high priest (from the tribe of Levi) would enter the Holy of Holies once a year (with Blood) to atone (cover) for the sins of the Nation of Israel and bring reconciliation between God and the Israelites, but this would have to be done every year.

In Hebrews 9 it says that, "Christ (Jesus) came as a High Priest of the good things to come, entering a perfect tabernacle not made with human hands and not part of this material creation, but with His own Blood He entered the Most Holy Place once for all, having obtained eternal redemption!"

"Once for all!"

What Jesus did in Heaven two thousand years ago (or two days ago 2 Peter 3:8) will never have to be done again, His Blood was and is eternally sufficient!

Eternal Redemption

John 10:28-29, "I have given them eternal life, neither shall anyone snatch them from out of My hand! My Father has given them to Me and no one is able to snatch them out of My Father's hand!"

Ephesians 1:7 says, "In Him we have redemption (eternal) through His Blood. The forgiveness of sins (past, present and future) according to the riches of His grace!"

Revelation 1:5-6, "To Him who loved us and washed us from our sin in His own Blood and has made us kings and priests to His God and Father!"

David, the Warrior, Prophet and King says in Psalm 103:3-4, "Who forgives all our iniquities and who <u>redeemed</u> our life from destruction!"

If you are Born Again, then you have been eternally redeemed. Your redemption price was His (Jesus') Blood, and there is nothing Satan can do about it. The Blood of Jesus is all powerful and applied faith in the Blood will cause you to walk as one of God's "Untouchables". Dominion is the legal Blood bought right of the redeemed. Remember Satan has no defence against the Blood. You have been redeemed from:

1. Darkness into light.
2. Death into life.
3. Fear into faith.
4. Sickness into health.
5. Poverty into Prosperity.

"Study the Blood!"
"The Keys are in the Blood!"

I will end this Chapter with some declarations. It is essential, as the redeemed of God, that we confess with our mouth what we believe in our hearts. Hebrews 10:23 says, "Let us hold fast to our confession!" So, these declarations are to be said with bold, confident faith. As the redeemed, all the Heavens have been opened up to us by Jesus through His Blood. As the redeemed, we have eternal access to the Father! Hebrews 4:16, "Let us therefore come boldly to the Throne of Grace!" Hebrews 10:19, 23, "Therefore, having boldness to enter the Holies by the Blood of Jesus, let us hold fast our confession!"

Declarations!
In the name of Jesus,
and because of the Blood of the Lamb,
I declare that today I am engaging
and interacting with the realms of the
Holy Spirit and the dimensions of Zion!

I declare that I regularly see Angels,
interact with Angels,
hear Angels,
speak with Angels
and travel with Angels.

I declare that because of the Blood of Jesus,
I am having daily Throne Room encounters
and open visions.
The Holy Spirit is frequently
transfiguring and translocating me!

I declare in the name of Jesus
that I am a regular participator
in the Court Rooms of Heaven!

I declare that because of the Blood of the Lamb,
I daily engage with the Seven Spirits of God
and the Cloud of Witnesses!

I declare that, in the name of Jesus,
bi-location is a regular occurrence in my life!

I declare that by the Holy Spirit,
I regularly visit Heaven,
ride in the fiery chariots of God
and have international and inter-dimensional
Kingdom dreams!

I declare as a Blood bought,
Blood washed son/daughter of God,
I have a place of honour
in the House of Heroes!

**I declare because of the Blood of the Lamb,
ecstasies, trances, visions, revealed mysteries
and the discovery of unsearchable things
is my daily portion!**

**I declare in the name of Jesus,
and because of the Blood of the Lamb,
I am continually soaking in the oil of joy,
I am continually drinking
in the House of Wine
and I am continually filled
and overflowing with the
fire, power and glory
of my God and King Jesus!**

"As He is, so we are in this world, so let us rise up in our thinking and accept this amazing grace, favour and privilege that has been freely given to us by our Heavenly Father. The price that was paid so that we can experience days of Heaven on earth was the Blood of Jesus!"

"Confess with your mouth what you believe in your heart about the Blood of Jesus and watch your life and world be revolutionised by the Holy Spirit!"

10

The Righteous and the Favoured

When Jesus poured out His Blood (as God's High Priest, Hebrews 3:1) on the Mercy Seat in the Most Holy Place (Hebrews 9:12) two thousand years ago, the ransom price for the redemption of all humanity (the race of Adam) was paid in full (Ephesians 1:7). When a man or a woman puts their faith in Jesus (Romans 10:10), they are instantly washed (by the Holy Spirit) in the Blood of the Lamb (Revelation 1:5). This experience is called "The New Birth or being Born Again" (John 3:3, 7; 1 Peter 1:23). That person (because of the Spirit and the Blood) then becomes a new creation (2 Corinthians 5:17), but the amazing grace of God does not stop there. They also instantly enter into a "New Blood Covenant" (which includes all the protection, prosperity and blessings of all the old blood covenants) with Jesus himself as the guarantee of their fulfilment (Hebrews 7:22). Also, they are instantly connected up to the Jubilee (Luke 4:18). The two main concepts of the Jubilee are "FREEDOM AND RESTORATION!"

After being washed in the Blood of the Lamb we become "The Righteousness of God in Christ Jesus" (2 Corinthians 5:21).

Declaration!
(2 Corinthians 4:13)

I declare, because of the Blood of the Lamb,
I am the righteousness of God in Christ Jesus!

I declare, because of the Blood of the Lamb,
I have been ransomed
from the power of the grave!

I declare, because of the Blood of the Lamb,
I have been redeemed from death!

I declare, because of the Blood of the Lamb,
"By His wounds I am healed!"

"The Life is in the Blood!"

"The Keys are in the Blood!"
"Study the Blood!"

Once you are Born Again, all God's Blood Covenant promises about the righteous and righteousness become yours (not by works, but by faith). God's eternal decision about all His Blood Covenant oaths are "**YES AND AMEN**" (2 Corinthians 1:20). He is not as man that he should lie (Numbers 23:19). He has made Jesus your guarantee (Hebrews 7:22), but in order to appropriate these promises in our daily lives here on earth, the key ingredient is "Faith". "The just (righteous) shall live by faith" (Habakkuk 2:4c; Romans 1:17).

Declaration!

Because I am the righteousness of God,
Through and by the Blood of the Lamb
(Romans 5:9),
I live by faith!
(2 Corinthians 5:7)
I walk by faith!
I speak by faith!
(2 Corinthians 4:13)

Remember, Satan's kingdom is a counterfeit kingdom, but he cannot counterfeit the Blood!

There are many, many promises in the Word of God to the righteous (by Blood). In Psalms there are about sixty, in Proverbs fifty and also in the Psalms there are about seventy Blood Covenant promises concerning righteousness and twenty-one in Proverbs. That is an amazing two hundred plus Blood Covenant oaths made by God to us, His Blood bought, Blood washed sons and daughters! So, it would be good to look into some of these promises (ignorance is our enemy), start to appropriate them and speak them out by faith! Jesus went through unimaginable agony to get His word into our lives, so let us lay hold of these "Exceedingly great and precious promises" (2 Peter 1:4).

Let us start with Psalm 5:12. This Psalm was written by David, a warrior, prophet and king. He was a man after God's own heart and had a very intimate relationship with Yahweh! In verse 12 it says, "For you, O Lord, will bless the righteous; With favour You will surround (encircle) him (the righteous) like a shield!" If you are Born Again, then this scripture is talking about you, because you are righteous through and by the Blood of Jesus! So what does the word "bless" mean for you and me (the righteous)? The answer to that question is in Proverbs 10:22 which says, "The blessing of the Lord makes one rich (wealthy) and he adds no sorrow to it!" So, the blessing of God in the lives of His Blood Covenant sons and daughters is to financially prosper them and make them wealthy. This is a Blood Covenant promise!

In Genesis 15:1 God says to Abraham, "I AM your exceedingly great reward", so then those who are of faith (the righteous) are blessed with believing Abraham (Galatians 3:9), and remember, it is trouble free wealth!

There are two scriptures in Ecclesiastes that I believe fit perfectly in with Psalm 5:12, and they are Ecclesiastes 5:19 and 20. Taken by faith from this side of the Cross, they are specifically for the Blood washed, Blood bought, righteous sons and daughters of the Living God!

Ecclesiastes 5:19 says, "To every man (the righteous) to who God (Elohim) gives riches and wealth, (Neh-kes – to accumulate treasure, riches) and given him (the righteous) the power to eat of it, to receive his heritage and rejoice (saw-makh – brighten up, cheer up, be glad and be joyful) in his labour (the labour of faith Hebrews 4:11), for this is a gift (grace and favour) from God (Elohim). For he (the righteous) will not dwell unduly on the days of his life, because God (Elohim) keeps him busy with the joy of his heart!!!" If you are "The righteousness of God in

Christ Jesus" (through the Blood), not only does our King (Jesus) want you to abundantly (super abundantly, beyond measure John 10:10b) prosper, He also (according to Ecclesiastes 5:20) wants to keep you busy with the joy of your heart!

Joy is supernatural and a manifestation of the Holy Spirit (Galatians 5:22). It is also the supernatural strength (Nehemiah 8:10) that the Blood Covenant sons and daughters of God need in every part of their life, every day! Joy is also a Kingdom Key for accessing the "Wells of salvation!" (Isaiah 12:3)

We have been eternally ransomed, redeemed and made righteous through and by the Blood of Jesus. This legally entitles us (by faith not works) to all the "protection and prosperity" there is in the New Blood Covenant, with Jesus as our guarantee (Hebrews 7:22). Our Saviour is Jesus and our salvation comes through and by His Blood. The word "Saviour" is "Yesh-oo-ah". In Isaiah 12:3 it says, "With joy you shall draw water from the wells of salvation!" The wells of salvation, the components of salvation, in this scripture are "deliverance, aid, victory, prosperity, health and welfare!" So, if you take 2 Corinthians 5:21, Psalm 5:12, Ecclesiastes 5:19 and 20 and Isaiah 12:3, you will see that under the inspiration and guidance of the Holy Spirit, Paul, David, Solomon and Isaiah are all describing the eternal (Psalm 119:89), never changing will/word of our Heavenly Father towards those who are righteous (through the Blood) in His sight! It is our King's (Jesus') Will for us to live in "mega" prosperity, to be full and overflowing with joy, totally delivered, healed and victorious (dominion) in every area of our lives! "As He is, so are we in this world!"

These exceedingly great and precious promises (2 Peter 1:4) are ours through faith in the Blood and through application of the Blood! Faith without works is dead (James 2:26)! Having the Word of God in your heart is good, but if we don't release it audibly (2 Corinthians 4:13), then it can't produce after its own kind (Genesis 1:11; Matthew 13:3-9, 18-23). God said, "Let there be light" (Genesis 1:3) and light is what He got, not galaxies, planets, trees or tomatoes, He got what He said, "light"!

So, as Blood bought, Blood washed sons and daughters of God, we need to declare and decree (Job 22:28) boldly and courageously what the Blood Covenant says about us and what the Blood Covenant says about our legal Kingdom rights! Remember, Satan and his kingdom (Ephesians 6:12) cannot counterfeit the Blood. The New Blood Covenant that we are in has "unbreakable protection and unstoppable prosperity". All scripture is God breathed and is profitable for doctrine, reproof, correction and for instruction in righteousness (2 Timothy 3:16).

At this point in Chapter Ten, let us put together seven declarations about righteousness and favour!

Declaration!
(Romans 5:9; Proverbs 10:22)

I declare, in the Name of Jesus
and because of the Blood of the Lamb,
I am righteous,
and because I am righteous, I am blessed
and the blessing of the Lord is making me
rich, wealthy and prosperous!

Declarations!

I declare, in the Name of Jesus
and because of the Blood of the Lamb,
the favour of my God and King is upon my life
and with His favour comes His blessings
and the blessings of the Lord
are making me rich in every way!

I declare, in the Name of Jesus
and because of the Blood of the Lamb,
the favour, blessing and angels of God
are at work on my behalf today
and His favour goes before me,
opening doors of financial prosperity
that no one can shut!

I declare, in the Name of Jesus
and because of the Blood of the New Covenant,
the favour of my God and King,
which surrounds me like a shield,
is changing rules, regulations,
laws, policies and seasons,
so that I am always the head and never the tail,
always above and never below!

I declare, in the Name of Jesus
and because of the Blood of the Lamb,
the favour of God upon my life today
is giving me preferential treatment,
above, beyond and before all others!

I declare, in the Name of Jesus
and because of the Blood of the Lamb,
today is my Kingdom receiving day
and I fully expect manifestations of the Blessing,

Favour and Glory of my God and King
to come upon me and go before me today!

I declare, in the Name of Jesus
and because of the Blood of the Lamb,
I am highly favoured
and the divine favour of my King Jesus
is making my daily life,
light, easy, harmonious and extremely
prosperous!

Hebrews 4:14
"Seeing then that we have a great High Priest
who has passed through the Heavenlies,
Jesus the Son of God,
Let us hold fast to our confession!"

In the Word of God it states, "Let everything be established by two or three witnesses", so let us look at two very powerful scriptures that directly concern you, "the righteous"!

Psalm 72:7
"In His days the righteous shall flourish,
And have abundance of peace (shalom),
Until the moon is no more!"

<u>Proverbs 11:28</u>
<u>"The righteous shall flourish like a green leaf!"</u>

Remember, Jesus went through unimaginable pain and agony to set these exceedingly great and precious promises to us (2 Peter 1:4).

"Study the Blood!"

Now, let us look at the first statement in Psalm 72:7, "IN HIS DAYS", because whatever is said next in Psalm 72:7, is only going to happen "In His days". So, when are His days? The answer to the question is in Acts 2:21, 38, 39 and 2 Corinthians 6:2.

<u>Acts 2:21, 38, 39</u>
"It shall come to pass that
whoever calls on the name
(position, authority and character)
of the Lord,
shall be saved (delivered and protected).
Then Peter said to them,
"Repent and let everyone of you be baptised
in the name of Jesus Christ,
for the remission of your sins
and you shall receive the gift of the Holy Spirit,
for the promise is for you and your children

and to all who are afar off,
as many as the Lord our God shall call!"

2 Corinthians 6:2

"For He says, "In an acceptable time, I have heard you and in the day of salvation I have helped you. Behold, now is the acceptable time. Behold, now is the Day of Salvation (Deliverance, Victory, Health, Prosperity).""

So, by meditating (Joshua 1:8; Psalm 1:2-3) on these scriptures, it is plain to see that "IN HIS DAYS" started at Pentecost and we are now all living "IN HIS DAYS". "Today is the day the Lord has made", so it's about time the righteous stopped living below their Blood bought privileges and start to take our Heavenly Father at His Word!

Hebrews 3:12, 19, 4:2

"Beware, let there be any of you with
an evil heart of unbelief,
they could not enter in because of unbelief,
for the word they heard
did not profit them
not being mixed with faith
in those who heard it."

"IN HIS DAYS (NOW, TODAY), the righteous

(through His Blood, not by works) shall flourish!" It is the Will of our Father that His Blood bought, Blood washed, Spirit filled children **<u>FLOURISH</u>** in every area of their lives (in the visible and in the invisible), so it would be good to know (ignorance is our enemy) what the word "flourish" means.

To flourish means:
- To grow in a healthy and vigorous way!
- To grow and develop successfully!
- To show luxuriantly!
- To thrive!
- To fly!
- To prosper!
- To bloom!
- To spread out!
- To expand!
- To spring up!
- To break forth!
- To blossom!

It is extremely obvious as we look at the word "flourish" in Psalm 72:7 and Proverbs 11:28 that it is not the will of our Heavenly Father that His people who are righteous through the Blood of the Lamb should live a life of failure, poverty, shortage, lack, ruin, debt, confinement, containment or restriction. The Word is very clear, "**<u>We are to FLOURISH</u>**", and not only are we to flourish, we are also supposed to be experiencing (Psalm 72:7) abundant peace (shalom).

Let us take a quick look at the word "SHALOM":

- Safety
- Prosperity
- Restoration
- Restitution
- Welfare
- Happiness
- Health
- Favour
- Rest
- Reward

This is amazing grace and exceedingly good news!

Let us now put together some declarations which will incorporate some of the definitions of the words "flourish and shalom"!

Declaration!

I declare that, because I am righteous through and by the Blood of Jesus, the Holy Spirit is causing me to grow and flourish in a healthy, vigorous and successful way!

**I declare, because of the Blood of the Lamb,
the Holy Spirit and the Angels of God
are causing me to prosper,
thrive and grow luxuriantly!**

**I declare, because of the Blood of the Lamb,
the Favour of God within and upon my life
is opening new dimensional doors of
financial prosperity, that no one can shut!**

**I declare, in the Name of Jesus
and because of the Blood of the Lamb,
the Holy Spirit and the ministering angels are
directing my thoughts, words and steps along
straight safe and secure financial pathways!**

"Study the Blood!"

I will end this Chapter with a reminder that all the promises (oaths) of God connected to the Blood Covenant are "**YES AND AMEN**", and all the promises in scripture about the righteous (through Blood not works) are also "**YES AND AMEN**"! Take them by faith, declare them by faith, and enjoy them by faith, because you (the righteous) are the apple of your Heavenly Father's eye!

11

"The Righteous Are as Bold as a Lion!"

One of the main character traits of the righteous is supposed to be "lion-like boldness", but sadly that doesn't seem to be the case in the Laodicean church of our time. The boldness is there (in their spirits), but pastorally centred churches do not train or encourage their people to walk as lions in the blood bought boldness, power and majesty of "The Lion of the Tribe of Judah"! So, let us look at where we live. We are multi-dimensional beings, new creations, citizens of Heaven and part of a Holy (through Blood) Nation. Let us narrow all that down to two statements:

1. We live in the visible;
2. We live in the invisible;

and, because the subject of this book is "THE BLOOD", let us look first at our lives in connection with Isaiah 32:18.

Remember, the two main components in a blood covenant are "PROTECTION and PROSPERITY!" Isaiah 32:18 is another Blood Covenant oath to the people of God (the righteous).

"STUDY THE BLOOD!"
"THE KEYS ARE IN THE BLOOD!"

Isaiah 32:18, "My people will dwell in a peaceful (shalom) habitation. In secure dwellings and quiet resting places!"

In order to qualify for the Blood Covenant Protection and Prosperity connected to this scripture we have to be one of "HIS PEOPLE", and from this side of the Cross, the only way that can happen is through "circumcision of the heart" (Romans 2:29), or another way of saying it is, "You must be Born Again" (John 3:3). At the new birth (through the Blood, by the Spirit) we instantly become "righteous", that qualifies us to be "His people". So, if you are Born Again you are "Righteous", and if you are "righteous", then

Isaiah 32:18 is talking directly to you! Jesus paid the price (IN BLOOD) and sent the Holy Spirit so that Isaiah 32:18 would become a living daily reality to the life of "His people".

Let us now open up Isaiah 32:18, "My people (the righteous) shall dwell (live) in peaceful (shalom – safe, prosperous, healthy, happy, favoured) habitations (homes). In secure (safe, protected and unbreachable) dwellings (homes) and in quiet (tranquil) resting places (free from fear, anxiety, hostility or intimidation)."

In Matthew 11:12 our King, Jesus states that the Kingdom of Heaven is forcefully advancing. This is because we have an enemy (Ephesians 6:12) who is illegally squatting on our territory, so in James 4:7 we are told:

1. Submit to God.
2. Resist the devil.
3. He will flee!

Submit to God in my life is to do what He says and for me to know His will. I need to pray/sing in tongues until I receive a strategy from the Holy Spirit, then apply it vigorously in the direction of the enemy!

Personal Testimony

In 1989 my wife and I moved from our City (under the direction of the Holy Spirit) thirty-five miles north, to a picturesque (only on the surface) town with a population of only just 8,000 people. The Holy Spirit moved us there to be part of a work that was being done by one of the charismatic churches in the town. We were offered a house on the far north side of the town (this was a place which the tourists never went to, ever saw or were told about). This particular area was a place of great lawlessness. The police force of this particular town would not enter the area and nobody from any of the town's churches would go there. This was demon territory and the spirit of lawlessness was ruling and reigning. So, we moved in! We put our two young sons into the local school.

The Holy Spirit gave me the strategy (the correct approach in achieving the desired targeted purpose) and it was to get up at 5.30am and start to walk the area and pray in strong focussed tongues. So, that is what I did, and all the devils in the area got really upset. There were more stabbings, beatings, rape threats, drug using and dealing and a lot of drunkenness, but I had been given the strategy by the Holy Spirit and I wasn't going to stop, and Isaiah

32:18 was a Rhema promise from my King to me and my family!

So, I carried on praying in tongues and walking the area at 5:30 in the morning. Over a period of time (about nine months) the atmosphere began to change. It became less hostile, people started to be evicted, moved out or were put in prison. It was the first sign of the particular area becoming a peaceful habitation. New people and families started to move in. The area was being transformed by the Power of God. The spirit of lawlessness had been evicted and the police started to visit the area. It was safe to walk the streets again! We moved back to our City in 1990, job done!

The Rhema Word of God in the mouth of a Blood Covenant son or daughter of God cannot be stopped or resisted by the enemy. The fervent prayers (tongues) of a righteous man or woman makes tremendous power available!

"Do not live below your Blood Covenant Privileges!"

<u>Declaration</u>

I declare, in the Name of Jesus
and because of the Blood of the Lamb,
I am the righteousness of God in Christ,
and as a Citizen of Heaven,

it is my Blood bought right to live here on earth in a safe, secure, healthy and prosperous environment!

"Study the Blood!"
"The Life is in the Blood!"
"The Keys are in the Blood!"
"Get the Blood to the Body!"

Isaiah 32:18 can be a daily increasing reality in the lives of every Blood bought believer, no matter what the circumstances are, but, once again, it is a lack of lion-like boldness and courage in the average Christian that keeps them bound and immobilised! The spirit of religious witch-craft (this will be explained upon later in this book) intimidation (see Chapter 6). Compromise and passivity are illegally ruling and reigning in the church. Our King (Jesus) is calling His people "out" to join the resistance and to stand with Him and the Ecclesia and drive the devils out of His body!

There are two powerful forces that work in the lives of every human being (seven billion) on earth, and they are "HUNGER and ANGER"! Hunger will cause a person to "get up and move", and anger will empower a person to "rise up and fight"!

Isaiah 32:18 is talking to us about our home lives and

environments. If we want change, then we need to allow the Holy Spirit to fill us with His "righteous anger", and go on the attack!

"Attack is the best form of defence!"

Righteous anger is the birth place of Kingdom solutions! Situations change when anger is born (John 2:15-17). Jesus made a whip out of three cords (symbolic of the bench of three) and entered the temple and violently threw everyone and everything out! In verse 17 it says, "Zeal for my Father's house has eaten me up!" Let's expand this verse, "Red hot burning jealously for my Father's house has totally consumed and devoured me!"

When Jesus entered the temple with the whip (which was a weapon in His hand), His spiritual, mental, emotional and physical state was one of "red hot burning jealously" (remember Jesus only ever did what He saw His Father doing). Anger requires focus. Do not let the spirit of religious witchcraft keep you out of your Blood bought Kingdom promises and destiny. Isaiah 32:18 concerns your home and your environment and it is your legal right (through the Blood by faith) to experience Heaven on earth.

What you tolerate will dominate!

**What you compromise to keep you lose!
You cannot correct
what you are unwilling to confront!**

So, after returning to the City in 1990, let us travel forward in time to 2002 and this is a testimony from my wife Linda.

In 2002, a demonically planned situation occurred which caused a lot of hostility and anger towards our fourteen year old daughter. At this time Paul and myself had paid for and planned for two nights away (something that we did not do very often), so we were looking forward to it.

However, we both believed that it was not safe for us to go and leave our daughter in this situation. We had been given dominion by the Holy Spirit in and for our area and to leave at this time would be handing it over to the enemy. We agreed to stay at home, even if it meant losing all the money that had been paid for the Hotel. We contacted the Hotel to say we could not come, but they said that they would honour our booking and we could go another time without any other payment required.

So, we received our strategy from the Holy Spirit to walk and pray in tongues from our home and the streets connected to our house. Also, we were told to speak directly to the spirits of anger and hostility (that wasn't their names, but their job description) and drive them out with our words! We also received a strategy on how to diffuse the whole situation on a natural level, and within forty-eight hours the atmosphere had changed, the situation had been resolved and once again the power of the Blood had brought deliverance and reconciliation!

"Study the Blood!"

Let's move on to another testimony. This is from JA and it happened on the 20th February 2021.

"The other day mam said she felt an unpleasant atmosphere in my brother's room. I got a word of knowledge that my brother had received some books from his teacher. I then received a vision of one of his books. I described it as a book with a man on a horse, on a yellow hill, dressed in Napoleon gear. My brother showed me the book and it was exactly as I had described it (I had never seen the book before). We then prayed the Blood over all his books and we were very aware of the demonic resistance, but it was removed! Afterwards mam and everyone else in the house felt that the atmosphere was back to normal!

The last four testimonies in this Chapter have been

about areas and houses, so let us put together some declarations which will incorporate Isaiah 32:18.

Declarations

I declare, in the Name of Jesus
and because of the Blood of the Lamb,
my house and the area that I live in
is demon free, sickness free and fear free!

I declare, because of the Blood of the Lamb,
my home is a safe and secure dwelling place!

I declare, in the Name of Jesus
and because of the Blood of the Lamb,
my home and my area are peaceful,
prosperous and protected by Warrior Angels!

"As He is, so are we in this World!"

We have been looking at Isaiah 32:18 in regards to homes, areas and environments. Now, let us look at the same scripture in regards to our physical bodies. Remember Isaiah 32:18 is a Blood Covenant promise (oath) to the righteous, Jesus is our guarantee and God never lies!

Your body is the house/home or dwelling place of your spirit. As a Blood bought, Blood washed son/

daughter of the living God, it is your legal right (based on the Blood Covenant) to dwell and live in a body that is demon free, sickness free and fear free! Everything that Jesus went through was so that "His people" could live, move and have their being in total freedom!

"It is for freedom that Christ has set us free!"

Before we are Born Again we have no defence against demonic oppression or infiltration, but once we give our lives to Jesus we can, in His Name, be delivered from all enemy activity in our minds and bodies. I have learnt through personal experience that the presence of the Holy Spirit (anointing) is essential for setting Christians free from the internal influence of demons and from external demonic oppression.

<u>Isaiah 10:27</u>

The yoke (demonic activity) will be destroyed because of the anointing.

<u>Psalm 97:3, 5</u>

A fire goes before him and burns up his enemies!

**The mountains (demonic strongholds)
melt like wax at the presence of the Lord!**

Micah 1:4b

The mountains will move under him.

Luke 4:18

**The Spirit of the Lord is upon me,
because he has anointed me
to set at liberty those who are oppressed!**

Next is a testimony from MD, 4th March 2021.

"I have been praying and declaring for a "brain washing" ever since I started to hear about the Blood of Jesus. Last night I knew that something was in me and it had to come out. When the drums started playing, the power of God came upon me, I fell to the floor and started to experience convulsions, but when L and E started to pray for me my body was rigid and the heat was profound. I heard L declare "Get out of her nervous system". Then there was an amazing white light and the demon spirit left. I believe that it gained entry during sixteen years of domestic abuse. Today I have such a clear mind, it is truly amazing grace!"

Our bodies are the temple of the Holy Spirit (1 Corinthians 6:19; 2 Timothy 2:20, 21). There should be only two spirits in the body of a believer; their Born Again spirit, and the Holy Spirit, but in my thirty-five years of Kingdom experience, this is not the case. There is a tremendous need for deliverance in the body of Christ!

<u>**Joel 2:32 and 3:16**</u>

For in Mount Zion and Jerusalem,
there shall be deliverance!

The Lord will roar from Zion!

<u>**Amos 1:2**</u>

The Lord roars from Zion!

<u>**Obadiah**</u>

On Mount Zion there shall be deliverance!
Deliverance shall come to Mount Zion
to judge the mountains of Esau!

The removal of demons from the lives, bodies and minds of God's Blood Covenant people is a direct demonstration of the Kingdom of God!

<u>**Luke 11:20**</u>

Jesus said, "If I cast out demons (from my people)
by the finger (power) of God,
surely the Kingdom of God
has come upon you (God's people)."

Wild beasts, reptiles and unclean birds should not be living in the people of God or the body of Christ here on earth. God's people are bound because God's leaders are bound. It is time for the Ecclesia to **rise up** and allow the Lion of the Tribe of Judah to ROAR through them by the Holy Spirit and set His people free! It is time to sharpen our swords (the Rhema Word), oil (anointing) our shields (faith) and go on the offensive (forcefully advancing His Kingdom). As Blood bought, Blood washed sons and daughters of God, it is our Blood Covenant right to be free!

A demon is a representative of another kingdom. Its purpose (one of many) is to stop or hinder God's people from fulfilling their destiny here on earth or to stop them (you) from having any type of testimony about the Blood, because it says in

Revelation 12:11
We (the righteous)
overcome him (Satan/demons)
by the Blood of the Lamb
and the Word (Rhema) of our testimony
(what the Blood has,
is and will eternally do for us).

"The Life is in the Blood!"
"The Keys are in the Blood!"
"Study the Blood!"
"The Blood Speaks!"

I said earlier most of God's people are bound because their leaders are bound and one of the main spirits Satan has sent against Blood bought, Blood washed leaders is the spirit of religious witchcraft. Personally I had to learn the hard way about this devil and how it works in the lives of leaders and believers, but its exposure and its influence in the body of Christ is essential for the deliverance of God's people in great numbers!

Religious Witchcraft

The purpose of religious witchcraft is to stop or attack and destroy the true ministry and voice of the apostle in the body of Christ (remember not everyone who says they are an apostle are actually an apostle). The strategy of religious witchcraft is to:

1. Infiltrate (Revelation 2:20a)
2. Contaminate (Acts 16:17)
3. Seduce (2 Kings 9:30; Revelation 2:20b)
4. Take control (Inheritance) (1 Kings 21:1-16)

The spirit of religious witchcraft targets the minds (1 Kings 19:2-4) and emotions of God's leaders in order to hinder or derail the advancement of God's Kingdom in and through them! This particular spirit and the demons it governs target breakthrough leaders and the governmental church (Ecclesia) because they pose a direct threat to the illegal, demonic influence that this demon has in, on or over the church!

The spirit of religious witchcraft will always try to exalt itself through human effort.

Jeremiah 2:13
My people have committed two evils;
They have forsaken Me,
the fountain of living waters,
And hewn themselves cisterns,
broken cisterns that can hold no water.

Hosea 5:11
Ephraim (double fruit)
is oppressed (violated, deceived)
and broken (crushed, discouraged) in judgement,
Because he (they) willingly walked by
human precepts (commandments).

Hosea 7:8-9
Ephraim has mixed (mingled)
himself (themselves)
among the people (nation);
Ephraim is a cake unturned.
Aliens (demons) have devoured his strength,
But he does not know it! (Hosea 4:6)

At this moment in time, religious witchcraft is making large inroads into the area of the prophetic and prophetic teaching. Its purpose is to silence and lockdown the Apostolic move of God in this century! Remember Satan has all the time we give him! (This portion of Chapter Eleven is being written on the 5th March 2021, thirteen months into the Chinese Flu, false lockdown, ineffective masks and antisocial distancing. What is commonly known as the five-fold ministry is nowhere to be seen in my region (about three million people) apart from on a two-dimensional computer screen.)

The spirit of religious witchcraft wants to be elevated to a position of power, influence and recognition in the church, so over a period of time it will draw people around itself leading and seducing them into deception and sin.

"The spirit of religious witchcraft must be confronted, overcome and removed!"

"<u>Church covens must be dismantled!</u>"

"Our King wants His people free!"

The spirit of religious witchcraft in the church has God's anointed leadership targeted (apostles or emerging apostles are at the top of its hit list). Its strategy is to:

1. Deceive, seduce, control, discredit (to make powerless).
2. Intimidate, discourage, cause loss of vision, confusion, disorientate and withdraw (to make powerless).
3. Oppression, depression, despair, hopelessness and perceived defeat (to make powerless).

This snake and everything connected to it must be crushed beneath the feet of the apostolically led Ecclesia and driven out by the fire of God.

Testimony

Linda and myself were part of a growing church that was moving in Kingdom praise/prayer, the gifts of the Spirit, angelic visitations, evangelism and the grace and favour of God was upon them. The senior leader was an apostle of God and very anointed, but religious witchcraft entered the work, deceived and seduced the senior apostle, who committed adultery, left his wife, two daughters and the Church. The work collapsed and many people were hurt. This testimony is not unique. Satan has no new plans to take out God's leaders because the ones he has still work!

Lastly, if the spirit of religious witchcraft can't intimidate you, it will turn its attack to praise and flattery,

"Guard your heart!"

Declarations

1. **In the Name of Jesus, I renounce and resist all and any involvement with the spirit of religious witchcraft. I plead the Blood over every part of my soul, mind and emotions. I declare that my heart and mind are guarded by the fire of the Holy Spirit!**

2. **In the Name of Jesus and because of the Blood of the Lamb, I break every satanic prayer and curse directed towards my life.**

3. **In the Name of Jesus and because of the Blood of the Lamb, I break every satanic challenge and assignment against my life.**

4. **In the Name of Jesus and because of the Blood of the Cross, I break every satanic desire and decree against my life!**

5. In the Name of Jesus and because of the Blood of the Lamb, I break every ungodly decree against my life!

6. In the Name of Jesus, my Apostle and great High Priest, I break every satanic plan formed in the Heavenlies against my life and destiny!

7. In the Name of Jesus and because of the Blood of the Lamb, I break every earthly demonic plan against my life and destiny!

These seven declarations are guidelines. Pray in tongues over them and ask the Holy Spirit for personal ones for you, your family and your sphere!

"Praying in tongues is a key
that opens the way for divinely inspired thought
and the apostolic Word of God!"

The Armour of God

The armour of God is a gift of grace to those who are righteous through and by the Blood of Jesus! When a person is Born Again there is a change of armour and weapons.

1. The belt of lies for the Belt of Truth!

2. The breastplate of unrighteousness for the Breastplate of Righteousness!

3. The shoes of torment for the War Boots of Peace (Shalom)!

4. The shield of unbelief for the Shield of Faith!

5. The helmet of damnation for the Helmet of Salvation!

6. The sword of Satan, which is the word of death, for the Sword of the Spirit, which is the Word of God!

Our King is calling His righteous sons and daughters to "**rise up**" in the power of the Holy Spirit and to "**step out**" in bold lion-like courage and evict the illegal squatters (demons) that are living in their territory (soul, minds, bodies and spheres) and witness the glorious victory that Jesus appropriated for us at the Cross, apply His Blood and see His Kingdom come!

Remember,

The righteous are as bold as a lion!
Our lives are hidden in Christ!
We are called to be His untouchables!

12

The Call

Everyone (no matter who you are) if you are reading this chapter then "You have been called!"

The first calling for me was "You must be born again", and that was on the 10th August 1985. The next calling was "Do you want to be baptised in the Holy Spirit and speak in tongues?" That was on the 11th August 1985. Then in September 1985 I heard very clearly the voice of the Holy Spirit (in the solar plexus area of my chest) say, "You must be baptised in water and take the bread and the wine", and that is what I did. I was baptised (full immersion) in a local Brethren Assembly in the east end of my City and I took the bread and the wine with the Anglicans.

"Obedience is better than sacrifice!" (Isaiah 1:19)

If you look back over your own journey you too will be aware of a number of callings from God that have (or could have) affected your life and direction, but every Born Again man or woman who has ever lived or will ever live on planet earth has received a call, and it is the same call (all the righteous are called with the same call) and it is found in Isaiah 42:6-7, "I, the Lord, have called You in righteousness!"

God's call is upon the lives of every Blood bought, Blood washed son and daughter of God. This call is a Blood Covenant call and it was initiated by Jesus, the Lord of our lives, the King of all kings, the Lion of the Tribe of Judah, the Alpha and the Omega, and the one who has the Name (position, authority, character) above all names! We have been called in righteousness, and all the Blood Covenant promises to "the righteous" and about "righteousness" are ours "IN CHRIST", they are eternally "Yes and Amen!"

The righteous are called to advance the Kingdom. They (we) are not called to join a church and advance a religious system or denomination! We must allow the Holy Spirit to disconnect and deprogramme our minds, belief systems, and fallen DNA from generational, religious Christianity, false denominational loyalty and religious witchcraft!

This would now be a good place to briefly mention familiar spirits.

FAMILIAR SPIRITS

A familiar spirit is a spirit that knows a person, place or system intimately. This type of spirit becomes intimately interwoven and accustomed over generations to the lifestyle, moods and behaviour patterns of the person/or system it inhabits. When a familiar spirit is in operation, the person or persons believe they are exercising their own free will. In reality they are being deceived and manipulated, they are blind to the enemy's activities within and through their lives. A familiar spirit works in, through and around a person's character (soul and mind). A familiar spirit knows the strengths and weaknesses that are in a person or system, and they exploit them in order to bring about the plan and strategy they have for that person or system.

John 10:10

The devil comes to steal, kill and destroy!

Familiar spirits influence and manipulate emotions and seek to control and dominate thought patterns.

They know how a person will react in any given situation. They know a person's comfort zones and their explosive zones. Familiar spirits are residential spirits. Familiar spirits are generational and geographical, they become very uncomfortable and agitated when they perceive they are going to be moved from their particular home or area.

Mark 5:10

And they begged Jesus again and again not to send them out the area!

Familiar spirits will fight against change and will cause the person or system they inhabit to fear and resist change.

Denominational religion is the home of many types of familiar spirits. Religious rituals (from the Catholic to the Charismatic) which cannot or will not be changed are governed and infested by familiar spirits. Just as in the natural we take on the physical look of our parents or grandparents, eg eye colour, shape of nose, colour of hair, we are also born with similar personality traits and it is in the personality (soul and mind) where familiar spirits reside.

Familiar spirits do not want the person or system they inhabit to know the truth.

John 8:32
You will know the truth
and the truth will set you free!

When a person is Born Again, that is when (as the righteousness of God) they can start their own personal attack against the familiar spirits that have contaminated their lives.

When familiar spirits are exposed they must be dealt with powerfully and permanently.

Job 12:22
He reveals the deep things of darkness
and brings deep shadows into the light!

Hebrews 4:13
Nothing in all creation
is hidden from God's sight.
Everything is uncovered
and laid bare before His eyes!

The will of our Father is that His Blood bought, Blood washed sons and daughters (the righteous) live lives that are totally free. The only spirit we are to be familiar with is the Holy Spirit, so "let there be light and let us move from Glory to Glory!"

Jesus came to restore everything Adam lost, and when

we put our faith in Jesus and we are Born Again and become the righteousness of God through the Blood of the Lamb, the mandate (an official order or commission to carry out an assignment) that God (Elohim) gave Adam became ours!

Let us quickly look at the sevenfold mandate that God gave Adam, and Adam and Eve.

The Adamic Mandate

Genesis 2:15	Genesis 1:28
1. Cultivate	3. Be fruitful (Reproduce)
2. Protect	4. Multiply (Increase)
	5. Replenish the earth (Refill)
	6. Subdue the earth (Conquer)
	7. Have dominion (Rule)

There is nothing passive or religious about these seven statements. As Blood bought, Blood washed, Blood Covenant sons and daughters of God, we need a significant download from the Holy Spirit about the practical application (in the visible and the invisible) of the "Adamic Mandate".

Under the direction of the Holy Spirit, the "Adamic Mandate" is now the responsibility of the righteous!

The earth is ours, Psalm 115:16 says, "The earth has

been given to the children of men!" If we (the righteous) continue to allow Satan and his government (Ephesians 6:12) to run and direct planet earth (in the visible and the invisible) through the unredeemed and the religious, then mankind, the church and planet earth will be in a continuous cycle of increasing chaos, fear and confusion!

The earth is ours and "When the righteous are in authority, then the people rejoice!" (Proverbs 29:2a) Another word for authority is "dominion". Jesus came to restore to all who would put their faith in Him, their own "personal dominion!"

Personal dominion is the base and launchpad for every other form of dominion (in the visible and the invisible). Our Heavenly Father wants mature sons and daughters (watched over by the Holy Spirit and mentored by the Seven Spirits of God) to rule and reign on His behalf!

One of the main strongholds I've come across in the last thirty-five years that opposes personal dominion is <u>GUILT</u>.

"GUILT IS NOT FROM GOD!"

Jesus our King, after His resurrection, did not

commission guilt to be one of the motivational forces to advance His kingdom.

"GUILT EVANGELISM IS NOT FROM GOD!"

Apostles, prophets, evangelists, pastors, teachers and parents who use guilt to get things done are a mouthpiece for an anti-Christ demon. The Kingdom of God in the Heavenlies and on earth and every realm and dimension connected to them is supposed to be advancing in the power of the Holy Spirit through and by mature sons and daughters of God who live, walk and talk faith, not guilt.

It is impossible to be righteous (through the Blood of Jesus) and be guilty in the eyes of God at the same time!

"Study the Blood!"

When a man or woman asks Jesus into their lives, they are washed in the Blood of the Lamb. All their sins (past, present and future) are eternally erased through and by the Blood! The Blood of Jesus makes you one hundred percent righteous, twenty-four-seven! There is never a time (awake or asleep) when a son or daughter of God is not righteous in His sight!

Our righteousness did not, does not or never will be because of what we have done or ever will do.

Statement: Righteousness is an eternal gift of grace from a loving Father!

"Study the Blood!"
"The Life is in the Blood!"
"The Keys are in the Blood!"

The source of guilt is satanic and the purpose of guilt is to cause the righteous (those who are eternally not guilty) to feed daily from the tree of the knowledge of good and evil, which always produces death (powerlessness) and to be a people of worry instead of a supernatural people of the Spirit!

Guilt and religion go hand in hand! Jesus did not come to planet earth to restore a religion. Adam never lost a religion, Jesus came to restore "dominion"!

The Kingdom of God and religion are in direct opposition to each other, and I am not talking about Hinduism, Buddhism or Islam. The biggest problem this earth has is the religion of Christianism, it has a form of godliness, but no power. The purpose of religious Christianism is to "conform and control" and guilt is a major player in this process!

In Romans 1:17, Galatians 3:11 and Hebrews 10:38 it says, "The righteous shall live by faith." It does not say, "The righteous shall live by guilt." The guilt issue is made clear in Hebrews 10:2 and it is because guilt is a product of a consciousness of sin, or a sin consciousness! It is only the Blood and faith in the Blood of Jesus that can turn a person's mind from sin consciousness to a righteousness consciousness!

As sons and daughters of God who are righteous (eternally not guilty) through the Blood of the Lamb, we need to yield our soul, mind and DNA to the Holy Spirit so that He can purge us from guilt and flood us daily with a heavenly awareness of the righteousness which is ours through the Blood.

Declaration

**I declare that, because of the Blood of the Lamb,
I am eternally righteous and free
from all condemnation and guilt!**

I am the righteousness of God!

Now let us open up Isaiah 42:6-7.

"I, the Lord, have called YOU (the righteous) in righteousness!"

I will hold (grasp and strengthen) Your hand

(YAWD – power, means, direction, force, ministry and dominion). I will keep (NAW-TSAR – guard, protect, manage, hide and preserve) <u>You</u> and give and restore <u>You</u> as a Blood Covenant gift to my people (the righteous) and as a light (fire, illumination) to the Gentiles.

To open (awaken) blind (closed) eyes, to bring out (YAW-TSAW – bring forth, breakout, carry out, to pull out) prisoners (bound captives) from prison and those who sit (have given up) in darkness (KHO-SHAK – misery, sorrow, ignorance, wickedness, destruction, obscurity and death) from the prison (family, dungeon, place)."

"The righteous are as bold as a lion!"

The very moment we are Born Again, this call also becomes ours. We may not have realised it at the time (I didn't), but ignorance is the enemy of destiny (Hosea 4:6). Every Born Again man or woman is called to walk out and implement Isaiah 42:6-7 wherever, whenever and however the Holy Spirit directs!

Isaiah 42:6-7 is not a call or ministry for the special few, just as Mark 16:15-18 is not a call or ministry for the special few. They are both the call of God and the ministry of the King of kings upon the lives of His

Blood Covenant people (the righteous). Whether you've been baptised in the Holy Spirit or not isn't the issue, this is a Blood Covenant call not a special anointing. You (the righteous) have been hand picked by the King of kings (John 15:16) to advance His kingdom. So,

"Get Up, Look Up and Step Out!"
"As He is, so are we in the world!"

Just as Isaiah 42:6-7 and Mark 16:15-18 are very important directional scriptures for us (the righteous), there are another five sign post scriptures that need looked at.

1. Psalm 23:3
   Walk in the paths of righteousness!

2. Isaiah 32:17
   Do the work of righteousness!

3. 2 Corinthians 3:9
   Release the ministry of righteousness!

4. Daniel 12:13c
   Turn many to righteousness!

5. Isaiah 32:17b
   See the effects of righteousness!

So we have five men, David, Isaiah, Daniel, Mark and Paul, sent by God to tell us (the righteous) that whatever nation, culture, church or family we belong to, these words are for us. Now, let us take them by faith and see His Kingdom come and His will being done through us!

Declaration

I declare that, in the name of Jesus
and because of the Blood of the Lamb,
I am an ambassador of the Adamic Mandate and
I am walking in the paths of righteousness daily!

Declaration

I declare, because of the Blood of the Lamb,
the Holy Spirit is releasing through me
the ministry of righteousness!

Declaration

I declare, in the name of Jesus,
I am turning many to righteousness!

Declaration

I declare that, in the name of Jesus
and because of the Blood of the Lamb,
I am advancing God's kingdom,
casting out demons, speaking in tongues
and healing the sick!

<u>Declaration</u>

**I declare, in the name of Jesus,
that I am anointed with the
chain breaking, yoke destroying,
burden removing, stronghold demolishing,
cancer killing, pain removing,
snake crushing, sick healing,
prisoner releasing, debt erasing,
life giving power of Almighty God!**

"As He is, so are we in this world!"

The above statement is truly amazing and to qualify to be "as He is, in this world", it is very simple. It is attained by being righteous in the sight of God, through and by the Blood of Jesus. Not by works, but by faith!

Let us briefly look at some of the things He is, that we also are in Him! In Hebrews 1:3 it says that He (Jesus) is the exact mirror image and representation of the Father, so everything the Father is, Jesus is, and everything Jesus is, "we are"!

In order for everything we are in heaven to become a reality here on earth, we must "confess with our mouth, what we believe in our hearts!" Joshua 1:8 says, "Do not let my word depart from your mouth, but meditate on it day and night!" So, let us take some scriptures which declare who He is and turn them into personal declarations about who we are in Him!

Hebrews 1:3

Declaration

I declare, because of the Blood of the Lamb,
I am the mirror image and exact representation
of my Heavenly Father!

In John 1:7 it says that, "God is light", which also means, "Jesus is light", because we are in Him (Jesus), "We are light"!

Declaration

I declare, because of the Blood of the Lamb,
I am the "Light of God" in Christ Jesus!

In 1 John 4:16 it says, "God is love", which means "Jesus is love", and because we are in Him (Jesus), "we are love"!

Declaration

I declare, because of the Blood of the Lamb,
I am the "love of God" in Christ Jesus!

In Hebrews 12:29 it says our God is a "consuming fire", which means Jesus is also a "consuming fire", and because we are in Him (Jesus), we also are "consuming fires"!

<u>Declaration</u>

I declare, because of the Blood of Jesus,
I am the "fire of God" in Christ Jesus!

In 1 Peter 1:16 it says, "Be Holy, for I am Holy", because the Father is Holy, Jesus is Holy, and because we are in Him (Jesus), "we are Holy"!

<u>Declaration</u>

I declare, because of the Blood of Jesus,
I am the Holiness of God in Christ Jesus!

2 Corinthians 13:4 says, "He (Jesus) lives by the power of God", and because we are in Him (Jesus), we too are to live, move and have our being in the "power of God"!

<u>Declaration</u>

I declare, because of the Blood of Jesus,
I live, move and have my being
in the resurrection power of God!

God is the source of all life and in John 1:4 it says that, "In Him was <u>life</u>." Jesus is the way, the truth and the <u>life</u>, and because we are in Him (just as Jesus is one with the Father), we also are the "life of God"!

Declaration

**I declare, because of the Blood of Jesus,
I am the eternal, indestructible
life of God in Christ Jesus!**

So let us now put these seven declarations together and make them into one proclamation!

**"I declare, in the name of Jesus
and because of the Blood of the Lamb,
that I am the mirror image and exact
representation of my Heavenly Father.
I am the Light of God,
I am the Holiness of God,
I am the Fire of God,
I am the Power of God and
I am the Life of God.
As He is, so I am in this world!"**

"The Life is in the Blood!"

As chapter twelve is the last chapter of this book, let us finally look at "the bread and the wine" and "His flesh and His Blood"!

In the early part of this chapter, I mentioned that the Holy Spirit told me to "take the bread and the wine", which I did (by faith), although I had no understanding why, its amazing significance of its heavenly power! At this point I would like to thank Kenneth Copeland for his personal testimony about the bread and the wine. Many years ago (on a cassette tape), he talked about how he took the bread and the wine every week, and in times of trouble or negative pressure, every day. Until I heard his testimony, the bread and the wine was taken once a month in church. His testimony set my mind free from a religious, denominational lie!

Communion is meant to be a time of great celebration (collectively or individually), high praise, deliverance, healing and apostolic impartation!

After realising that I could take the bread and the wine (not counterfeit grape juice) anywhere, anytime, I asked the Holy Spirit a question and it was, "How can you take communion when there is no bread or wine available?" The answer came into my mind at lightning speed and it was, "By faith!" Little did I know that I was about to go on a journey that would take me behind the veil!

The scripture I was inspired to meditate (Joshua 1:8) on was John 6:53-56, so let us look at the words of Jesus, which are always the truth, the whole truth and nothing but the truth, because He is "the truth"!

<u>John 6:53-56</u>

Then Jesus said to them,
"Most assuredly I say to you,
unless you eat the flesh of the Son of Man,
or drink His blood,
you have no life in you.
Whosoever eats My flesh and drinks My Blood
has eternal life and,
I will raise him up on that last day.
For My flesh is food indeed,
and My blood is drink indeed.
He who eats My flesh and drinks My blood
abides in Me and I in him!"

In verse 66, John tells us that, "Many of His disciples went back and walked with Him no more." They couldn't handle the revelation, they took offence and left Him. It would be good to point out here that Jesus did not go chasing after them and try to get them to return. He let them go!

As I started to meditate on John 6:53-56, the question that was in my mind was, "How do I do this, how do I eat His flesh and drink His blood?" Once again the answer from the Holy Spirit was, "By faith!" This answer did not help, but it did motivate me to start to pray in tongues over John 6:53-56 and as I did I received a simple strategy and it involved my imagination. Isaiah 26:3 says that if you focus your imagination upon the Lord, he will keep you in perfect peace (shalom).

Imagination can help you create a reality in your mind (soul) before it becomes an experience in your world!

The Holy Spirit wants to restore your ability to day dream!

The strategy was this – I was to imagine in front of me on a plate, the flesh of Jesus (I pictured it looking like a piece of raw steak) and to imagine also in front of me a golden goblet full of the Blood of Jesus. So that is what I did. I would read out aloud John 6:53-56. Then I would pray or sing in tongues and picture in front of me the flesh and Blood of Jesus. This went on for a number of weeks (regularly, but not every day). I got to the place where all I had to do was shut my eyes and I could see the flesh and Blood of Jesus in front of me! Then the Holy Spirit took the process up another level and He said, "Take a piece of the flesh of Jesus and eat it by faith", which I did (this may seem strange to you, but life outside the religious box is where the action is). Then I did the same with the Blood of Jesus. Remember, Jesus said, "Eat my flesh, drink my Blood!" All through the process the enemy was trying to sow seeds of doubt in my mind, but overcomers do not give up, so I carried on and it wasn't long before the next stage of the process was revealed. One morning the Holy Spirit said, "Stand up and picture (imagine) in front of you a veil, then step through it!" So that is what I started to do, praying in tongues and imagining a veil in front of me and then taking a physical step forward! This act of faith produced an immediate result. I felt fire all over my body and my tongues changed.

Entering the Holy of Holies (Hebrews 10:19) is an actual event/encounter not a religious theory! The next part of the strategy was to "Take the body and the blood of Jesus after I stepped through the veil!"

"The righteous live by faith
And faith always produces a result!"

It has been a privilege to pass these strategies and the practice of them on to others, either individually or in a corporate setting (meeting). Once eating the body and drinking the Blood of Jesus becomes a heavenly habit, it can be done anywhere and at any time.

Testimony by MC in her own words

October 2019 – I was going to meet friends. I had been thinking of what Paul had said about taking the flesh and drinking the Blood of Jesus. He said, "You can take it anywhere, anytime!" So, on the Metro I pictured a table with the flesh of Jesus on a gold plate and a goblet containing His Blood. I started giving thanks praise (on the Metro) for His body, Blood, then I took them by faith. The next moment I was out of my body, outside of the Metro and in the Heavens, then within moments I was back in my body, very unexpected but a precious moment!

The above testimony could be described as an "ascension encounter!" Remember you are a spirit and your body is the home of your spirit. Your spirit is not under house arrest or lockdown, you can go out and come in at any time, by and through the Spirit!

Declaration

I declare, in the name of Jesus
and because of the Blood of the New Covenant,
I live, move and have my being
in ascension glory!

Testimony by NH in her own words

13/10/2020 – I was totally set free tonight! It was for freedom that Christ has set us free and it really happened tonight! What a breakthrough, eating the flesh and drinking the Blood of Jesus (John 6:53-56).

By faith Paul asked us to see the flesh of Jesus being

brought to us on a golden platter. We all took some and by faith ate it. Then His Blood came in a beautiful golden, jewel-encrusted goblet. We all drank!

WOW! The release! The freedom! I was released from a religious spirit that had entangled me for so long. It was a release from years of "doing" instead of being who I am meant to be!

John 6:56, "He who eats my flesh and drinks my blood abides in me, and I in him!"

John 15:7, "If you abide in me and my words abide in you, you will ask what you desire and it shall be done for you!"

Declarations

I declare, that as I eat the flesh
and drink the Blood of Jesus,
the Holy Spirit is renewing my mind
and restoring my soul!

I declare, that as I eat the flesh of Jesus
and drink the Blood of the Lamb,
my immune system is receiving a
supernatural upgrade by the Holy Spirit!

I declare, as I eat the flesh
and drink the Blood of Christ,
my nervous system is being restored
and renewed by the Holy Spirit!

I declare, that as I eat the Body of Christ
and drink the Blood of the Lamb,
the Holy Spirit is rejuvenating my youth
and upgrading my physical energy!

I declare, as I eat the flesh
and drink the Blood of Jesus,
ALL the blessings of the New Covenant
are being released by the Holy Spirit
into my life and delivered by the Angels!

I declare, as I take communion behind the veil,
I engage with the Seven Spirits of God,
the Seven Eyes of God,
the Seven Horns of God
and the Cloud of Witnesses!

I declare, as I eat the flesh
and drink the Blood of Christ by faith,
I am being transfigured from Glory to Glory
and days of Heaven on earth are mine today!

"The Life of the Flesh is in the Blood!"

I would now like to make a brief statement about "Water and Blood". Just as water has a powerful effect on our daily lives, so does the Blood of Jesus! Water can be used for washing and drinking. Washing is external, drinking is internal! Washing keeps us clean, drinking keeps us alive! So it is with the Blood of Jesus. Being washed in His Blood keeps us clean, but drinking His Blood will keep us alive and free from sickness, fear, demons and death! (John 6:53-54)

The Resurrection Life and Power of God is in the Blood of Jesus, so let us Drink Deeply and Live Free!

"The Keys are in the Blood!"

Let's now end chapter twelve with a scripture for all the wives, mothers and grandmothers, and it is Proverbs 31:21b and it says, "She clothed her household in scarlet!"

Apply the Blood to your household, your husband, children and grandchildren.

Apply the Blood to their places of work, their nurseries, schools and universities.

Apply the Blood to their social life and church life!

As a daughter of God and woman of righteousness, the Isaiah 32:18 life belongs to you, so apply the Blood to your households and watch as days of Heaven start to breakout in your world!

"Study the Blood!"
"The Keys are in the Blood!"
"Apply the Blood!"

My prayer for you is that, "The Lord will bless you (Proverbs 10:22), that He will enlarge your territory and extend your horizons, that you will be continually filled with the Holy Spirit and fire, and that you will know by revelation and experience what it is to "Eat His flesh and drink His Blood!""

SUMMARY

In summary I would like to draw your attention and imagination to the tremendous price that was paid by our King Jesus so that we could receive (by the Holy Spirit) revelation and experience of the Blood and the power and dominion that comes through and by the Blood! From the garden to the cross, a journey He took on our behalf so that we, through His Blood and faith in His Blood, could be reconciled to the Father, and receive and experience the "PROTECTION and PROSPERITY" that is ours through the New Blood Covenant!

Lightning Source UK Ltd.
Milton Keynes UK
UKHW020748200722
406119UK00009B/1030